THE
PURPLE
CROWN

Polyglossia: Radical Reformation Theologies

Edited by Peter Dula, Chris K. Huebner, and J. Alexander Sider

A series intended for conversation among academics, ministers, and laypersons regarding knowledge, beliefs, and the practices of the Christian faith, *Polyglossia* grows out of John Howard Yoder's call to see radical reformation as a tone, style, or a stance, a way of thinking theologically that requires precarious attempts to speak the gospel in new idioms. It is a form of theological reflection that blends patient vulnerability and hermeneutical charity with considered judgment and informed criticism. The books in this series will emerge out of conversations with contemporary movements in theology, as well as philosophy, political theory, and cultural studies.

THE
PURPLE
CR◉WN

Tripp York
Foreword by John D. Roth

The Politics of Martyrdom

Herald Press
Scottdale, Pennsylvania
Waterloo, Ontario

Library of Congress Cataloging-in-Publication Data
York, Tripp.
  The purple crown : the politics of martyrdom / Tripp York ; foreword by
John D. Roth.
      p. cm.
  Includes bibliographical references (p.   ) and index.
  ISBN-13: 978-0-8361-9393-0 (pbk. : alk. paper)
  1. Martyrdom—Christianity. I. Title.
  BR1601.3.Y67 2007
  272—dc22
                                          2007031764

To order or request information, please call 1-800-245-7894, or visit
www.heraldpress.com.

To my grandmother, Vivian Modena Seay (1918-2001), who made sure that every single time the church doors were open we were the first ones to walk through them, and to my mother, Joy York, who, well, at least made sure we got there.

When we pay honor to the martyrs, we are honoring the friends of Christ.

—Augustine

Contents

Foreword

Ever since its publication in 1660, *Het Bloedigh Tooneel*—better known to its English-speaking readers as the *Martyrs Mirror*—has been among the best-selling books in Anabaptist-Mennonite history. Thanks to the addition of Jan van Luycken's remarkable etchings in the Dutch edition of 1685 and its subsequent translation into English (1748) and German (1780), the *Martyrs Mirror* became a fixture in bookshelves of Amish, Mennonite and Hutterite homes throughout North America. Today the image of Dirk Willems—who returned to rescue his armed pursuer from the icy waters, and paid for it with his life—has become a kind of icon among Anabaptist groups; and the book's numerous stories of heroic, nonresistant witness to the way of Christ have made it a symbol of Christian faithfulness and Anabaptist-Mennonite identity.

Yet despite this sustained interest in the *Martyrs Mirror*, modern readers tend to be quite ambivalent about its central message. For those of us living in democracies—where Christian faith is more likely to evoke indifference than persecution—the stories of the *Martyrs Mirror* seem to come from a different age altogether. In a culture obsessed with preserving bodies and prolonging life, regardless of the cost, the ancient Christian discipline of "contemplating death" (*memento mori*) is not a highly popular theme. And we are far less confident than the martyrs about our grasp on Truth—the religious zeal that led Anabaptist parents to choose death over the needs of their children or inspired them to sing hymns as their bodies were burned strikes us as unsettling and extremist.

For anyone perplexed by the logic of Christian martyrdom or uncertain about its contemporary relevance, Tripp York's *The Purple Crown* merits a careful reading. Preparation for martyrdom, York argues in this illuminating book, is not the eccentric practice of a few religious zealots, but the basic posture of all Christians who have responded to the call to follow in the way of Jesus. Indeed, for the first three centuries after Christ, the early church simply assumed that martyrdom—that is, a willingness to accept death rather than renounce the faith or resort to violent weapons of self-defense—was the likely outcome of a disciplined Christian life. They prepared for death not as tragic victims but as witnesses (*martyrs*), whose patient suffering would give public testimony both to the fallenness of the world and to the ultimate victory of God over the powers of death.

As York makes clear, the martyr's witness is about more than just heroic steadfastness. Preparation for martyrdom, he suggests, is actually a form of public theology—a political act that fundamentally challenges and transforms standard assumptions about political life. Here York is responding to a strong tendency in Protestant ethical thought—represented most visibly in the work of Ernst Troeltsch and Reinhold Niebuhr—to dismiss any normative appeals to the imitation of Christ (*imitatio Christi*) or the Sermon on the Mount as "sectarian." Such an ethic might be naively charming in its idealism, but is ultimately irrelevant since public theology must deal with the weighty responsibilities of statecraft, justice and the judicious use of violence. By imposing a division between "political realities" and "religious ideals" these arguments assume that there is an autonomous space—the "secular" or the "political"—which somehow stands apart from the Christian narrative.

The witness of the martyrs, insists York, obliterates these distinctions. Through their patient, nonviolent suffering, Christian martyrs expose the futility of the logic of violence. At the same time, they bear public witness to the power of the resurrection and the triumph of Christ—the Lamb who was slain—as the rightful ruler over all nations and the end toward which all of history is ultimately moving. The politics of martyrdom is not a flight from the world. Instead, by appealing to the power of love over the fear of death, and the logic of persuasion rather than the violence of coercion, the martyr participates in a different form of politics—the politics of Jesus. As such, Christian martyrs—not princes, parliaments or presidents—are the true "bearers of history."

If you come to this book thinking that it is just another argument for "radical discipleship" or a martyr-driven guilt trip to promote "heroic Christianity," you would miss the most significant and exciting aspect of York's argument. In the end, the central goal of the Christian life is not martyrdom, but worship. All of the Christian life—from the smallest gesture of charity to martyrdom itself—is ultimately merely an expression of our deeper and prior desire for communion with God. And no part of worship, York claims, more fully expresses the joyful mystery of Christian faith than the celebration of the Lord's Supper, or the Eucharist.

Here, the theme of martyrdom becomes relevant for all Christians regardless of their circumstances. For in receiving the gift of Christ's body, broken for us, we participate in Christ's suffering and death, we engage the pain of the world, and we are saved from a disembodied Christianity. In celebrating the gift of Christ's body, resurrected for us, we participate in the promise of Christ's coming kingdom, we are empowered for joyful discipleship, and are saved from the politics of coercion and despair. Through worship Christians learn what it means to die well, and what it means to live well.

For those in the Anabaptist-Mennonite tradition, this book brings together a host of familiar themes even as it unsettles and inspires with its arguments regarding the centrality of worship. It will make you want to go back and re-read the *Martyrs Mirror*, if not for the first time, then with a fresh perspective. For those in the broader Christian tradition, this book will open up new perspectives on the political significance of worship. It will make you want to go back and re-read the Gospels for new insights into the politics of Jesus.

All readers will be confronted anew with the urgent relevance of Christian practices that point us toward the possibility of martyrdom—practices that remind us again that the ground of the martyr's hope, faith in Jesus Christ, is a transforming hope for all who wish to embrace it.

John D. Roth
Goshen College
August 2007

Acknowledgments

Alasdair MacIntyre is surely correct to suggest that we never start any-where. We simply find ourselves within a story that has been going on long before our arrival and will continue long after our departure. I am contemplating this position because I simply have no idea how to appropriately acknowledge all those people who, along the way, have enabled me to write this book, so I will name just a few.

I am indebted to the good people at Herald Press for taking a chance on me. Levi Miller has been a joy to work with, as well as the editors of the Polyglossia series: Peter Dula, Chris Huebner and Alex Sider. I had the good fortune of meeting the latter three as they were PhD students at Duke University while I was studying there. That they took me in and befriended what was an utterly confused fresh out of college graduate student means more to me than they can possibly imagine. Specifically, I am grateful to Chris for making this happen and to Alex for turning my manuscript into a readable book. Any mistakes are due to my obstinacy, not his careful suggestions.

While I was completing my PhD two of my colleagues, Andy Watts and Donna Techau, and two of my teachers, Kenneth Vaux and Brent Waters, were a vital source of help. They not only happily (most of the time anyway) tolerated my high-strung and imprecise theologizing but greatly added to the depth of my theological understanding. This book began with my dissertation and a committee George Kalantzius, Michael Budde, and Steve Long who provided invaluable suggestions and the kind of conversations that made writing this such a pleasura-ble experience. I am especially indebted to Steve whose manner of blending an Aristotelian approach to teaching while embodying a faithful account of Christian friendship constantly reminds me of why I wanted to study theology in the first place.

This book was completed during the end of my third year of teach-ing at Elon University in North Carolina. I am deeply appreciative to

13

both the scholars and the students in the Religious Studies Department for teaching me how to teach as well as for providing me the space to continue to work out these thoughts in a winter term course I taught on the history of Christian martyrdom. I am grateful to the students in that seminar for helping me to think better about this subject, and a special thanks in particular to Lauren Durr for her meticulous indexing of this book.

My parents, Fred and Joy York, have modeled what it means to provide good care for their family and neighbors. What has been taught to me by them goes beyond words and, thus, can only be imitated. Finally, to Tatiana Caban, whose care for animals, and this human animal in particular, is charity exemplified.

Tripp York
Feast of Ss. Hippolytus of Rome and Cassian of Imola
Anno Domini 2007

They say that a desert caravan, led by a Bedouin, was desperate with thirst and looked for water in the mirages of the desert. The Bedouin guided them, "Not there, but here." This happened several times. Finally, somebody got annoyed, took out a pistol, and shot the Bedouin. In his agony, the Bedouin stretched out his hand and said, "Not there, but here." And so he died, pointing the way.

Introduction

Martyrdom, Politics, Liturgy, and Discipleship

In *Being Political: Genealogies of Citizenship*, Engin Isin argues that citizenship renders political activity possible, yet is only realizable because of the noncitizen.[1] He argues that the barbarian, the slave, the woman, the alien, that is, any person or people excluded from citizenship, makes the category of citizenship intelligible. Isin bases his genealogy of citizenship on otherness, and this otherness opens the door for what it means, first, to be a citizen and, second, to have the ability to act upon such citizenship—that is, to be political.

Isin suggests that from the *polis* to the *civitas* a dialogical relationship is at work in the notion of citizenship and that this notion implicitly assumes an exclusion. There can be no account of citizenship if there is no account of those excluded from citizenship.[2] Therefore, whether in the ancient city-state or the modern nation-state, the city functions neither as the background nor as the foreground from which people garner their identity. The city is the *battleground* through which identity via citizenship occurs.[3] An account of otherness, therefore, must always be at work if one is to understand the true nature of what it means to be political.

Though an implicit antagonism is at work in such an account, early Christianity never had any qualms with viewing the world as a contest. Does it belong to God or does it belong to Satan? To which side does one belong, and which group will prove victorious by the game's end? This contest occurs at the very site where Isin argues that identity is procured: in the city. It is crucial, therefore, to be able to speak carefully about what constitutes Christian citizenship, the activities such citizenship (or lack thereof) presupposes, and how the Christian's status as a citizen (or noncitizen) does or does not determine her nature as a political creature. To expand upon Isin we must ask: Do martyrs, as the other, make politics a reality?[4] If so, the political case for martyrdom

17

becomes strong as politics is defined by what it is against—in this case, a specific group permanently banished, so to speak, from the city. Regardless of the answer one gives to the question, we must ask another: Must a Christian act on behalf of her citizenship in order to be political? If so, what does this mean in light of the dual citizenship that all Christians, via baptism, assume?

In *The City of God*, Augustine of Hippo argued that the reunification of creation depends upon Christians being faithful citizens. Almost sixteen hundred years later, Christians throughout the world are reminded that taking one's citizenship seriously, whether via voting or via serving in the military, is an inescapable duty. Citizenship affords one the ability to embody the kind of politics that can literally transform the world. For Christians to withdraw from politics would be tantamount to abandoning our responsibility for the well-being of the temporal order. Such abandonment would be not only apolitical but also poor Christian stewardship.[5]

Citizenship, and the responsible practice of it, is absolutely crucial for witness of the church. Christ victorious, the rule of Christ over all the nations, is, as the title of Oliver O'Donovan's political theology suggests, "the desire of the nations." O'Donovan argues that the "Christendom idea," so heavily criticized in post-Christendom liberalism, must be viewed under the lens of missiology—and the church is not at liberty to withdraw from its mission.[6] Christ is the rightful ruler of all the nations, and it is the church's task to remember such a rule and to embody it so that the world can know its genuine *telos* as a partaker in the divine economy that is the triune God.

However, what constitutes Christian citizenship? That is, what makes Christian citizenship different from non-Christian citizenship? One of the earliest Christian historians, Eusebius of Caesarea, told the story of the martyrdom of Sanctus, "who with magnificent, superhuman courage nobly withstood the entire range of human cruelty."[7] Regardless of the suffering Sanctus endured, he refused to offer his name, race, or birthplace. For him, these things were of little importance. To every question Sanctus was asked, he consistently replied with one answer: I am a Christian. "This he proclaimed," Eusebius noted, "over and over again, instead of name, birthplace, nationality, and everything else, and not another word did the heathen hear from him."[8]

The anonymous writer of the *Epistle to Diognetus* similarly privileges Christianity above nation and birthplace. The author enjoys the luxury of being able to spell out in further detail (than blessed Sanctus) the peculiar position of being a Christian in the world:

> Christians are distinguished from [others] neither by country nor by language nor by customs. For nowhere do they dwell in cities of their own; they do not use any strange form of speech or practice a singular mode of life. . . . But while they dwell in both Greek and barbarian cities, each as his [or her] lot was cast, and follow the customs of the land in dress and food and other matters of living, they show forth the remarkable and admittedly strange order of their own citizenship. They live in [their own countries], but as aliens. They share all things as citizens, and suffer all things as strangers. Every foreign land is [native to them], and every native land a foreign land. . . . They pass their days on earth, but they have their citizenship in heaven.[9]

The writer to Diognetus conveys the dual nature of citizenship for Christians. Christians share all things as citizens yet suffer as strangers; every land the Christian inhabits is treated as if it is her homeland, though it remains foreign to her; the Christian lives on earth, yet her true residency is in heaven. The Christian, therefore, makes do with what she finds on earth but does not hold it as having anything more than temporal status.

However, things have changed since the martyrdom of Sanctus. For one thing, whether for good or ill, Christendom happened. Constantine's Edict of Milan along with his later adoption of Christianity as the state religion, coupled with the emperor Theodosius making baptism a civil requirement, forever changed both the likelihood of martyrdom and the Christian's account of citizenship. When I speak of "the politics of martyrdom" in this book, I mean to trace this tension between the practice of citizenship and the possibility of martyrdom. To expand on Isin's account of alterity: does martyrdom make politics a possibility (through permanent exclusion from the city), or does the practice of Christian citizenship, rooted in the earthly city, eliminate the possibility of martyrdom?

Perhaps the theology of Augustine can help make some sense of this quandary.[10] To state briefly, for Augustine, being a faithful citizen meant that Christians are to embody the kind of citizenship that is outside the boundaries of temporal orders. That is, Augustine thought that faithful citizenship for Christians is, as the *Epistle to Diognetus* suggests, faithfulness to the politics of the heavenly kingdom. The Christian's journey through the earthly city is one of a pilgrimage through a foreign land— as her true citizenship resides in heaven. This journey, however, is not so much an escape from participation in "worldly" politics, as it is a radical interruption of the false politics located within the earthly city.[11] The earthly city, according to Augustine, cannot be an authentic *res publica* because there can be no true justice and no true charity where the triune God is not worshipped.[12]

Augustine's account of the city highlights a particular ground of agreement between both Constantinian and non-Constantinian theologians. That is, regardless of how theologians are positioned on the not-so-subtle shift of ecclesial dominance of the fourth century, we are all under the biblical command to seek the peace of the city (Jer 29:7). It is the manner in which we seek the peace of the city that divides us. Christians, ranging from Ignatius of Antioch to Jan Hus, from Menno Simons to Dietrich Bonhoeffer, have attempted to practice this command faithfully. Their paths are often quite different and, at times, conflict deeply. The one thing these divergent Christians share is the desire to seek the peace of the city in such a way as not to compromise who they are called to be. In this book I attempt to name what it means to be a part of a people required to embody this biblical command while remaining faithful to those things we know to be true.

It is tremendously hard, while seeking the peace of the city, to overcome the desire to *secure* that city's peace. "To seek" and "to secure" are not synonymous, and I contend that the Christian loses sight of the vision created by the incarnation of God when she attempts to guarantee such peace—as if it were something that could be controlled and manipulated. I find that the martyrs, as exemplary imitators of Christ, provide us with the means necessary to be able to know how we can seek the peace of the city without falling prey to the urge to ensure such peace (if such an "ensured peace" could be appropriately called peace). The martyrs exemplify life lived "out of control" inasmuch as they both entrust the loss of their lives to the memory of those who come after them and hope that such lives will be found worthy of eternal communion with God.[13] Such lives cannot want to take control of a world that Christians know is simply uncontrollable.

So the central task of the church is not to make Christianity the vessel by which world order is assured. Rather, by following Christ's command to witness to him, Christians expose the world *as world* to provide the world with a soteriological narrative. If it is true, as John Howard Yoder claims, that the church precedes the world epistemologically, then the world cannot even know it is the world unless the church is the church.[14] I will suggest that an authentic public theology, or a theology for the watching world, is grounded in the claim that the church (not the nation-state, market, or family) is the bearer of history.[15] This history, however, is a counter-history (or perhaps I should say "genuine" history), for it is predicated on those who follow the slaughtered Lamb. Eusebius of Caesarea stated it well:

> Other historians have confined themselves to the recording of victories in war and triumphs over enemies, of the exploits of the commanders and the heroism of their [soldiers], stained with the blood of the thousands they have slaughtered for the sake of children and country and possessions; it is peaceful wars, fought for the very peace of the soul, and [those] who in such wars have fought [dutifully] for truth rather than for country, for true religion rather than for their dear ones, that my account of God's commonwealth will inscribe imperishable monuments; it is the unshakeable determination of the champions of true religion, their courage and endurance, their triumphs over demons and victories over invisible opponents, and the crowns which all this won for them at the last, that it will make famous for all time.[16]

History, argued Eusebius, is made and recorded by those who reveal to the world its destined *telos*: worship of the triune God. The acts of the martyrs, along with the right recollection of these acts, constitute genuine history. William Bramley-Moore states that the "history of Christian martyrdom is, in fact, the history of Christianity itself."[17] If this is the case, martyrs, as 'champions of true religion,' are the bearers of history. The public and political implications indicative of such a claim suddenly become apparent.

By focusing on blood-witness as a crucial development of the term *mártus*, I suggest that the ability to produce martyrs requires an ecclesiology that assumes being a member of the body of Christ is political in nature.[18] To remember one's baptism is the most significant and truthful way one can be political, because it assumes that the very way that the church is in the world is a witness. This does not imply sectarianism or a privatization of the faith; rather it clarifies how Christianity differs from other narratives. The politics implicit within baptism denies the very distinctions that underwrite much of theology after modernity. Such distinctions include the split between the religious and the political, the body and the soul, and the sacred and the secular. The kind of theology *for* the public that I desire to articulate denies these distinctions in hopes of suggesting that the most responsible thing a Christian can do, for the world, is to be true to her baptism.

In his Gifford Lectures, Stanley Hauerwas claimed that the only legitimate argument Christians can make for the existence of God is that of being a witness.[19] For Hauerwas, evidence for God's existence comes not in the form of theories or proofs, but in the lives of those who claim that such existence is true. Our best argument, he suggests, is biographical. Following Hauerwas, I argue that "blood-witness" is the act by which those outside of (and within) Christianity recognize as significant the faithfulness of the one whom the church is called to reveal. This is important because it anticipates the way historical Christianity lays claim on contemporary Christianity. For example, why has the church in North America produced so few martyrs? What kind of church is ours if, in an era of gluttony, imperialism, avarice, and bloodlust, we cannot produce people who threaten such an order? Following Jesus may very well land us on a cross, and we should expect no less. The appropriate ecclesiological response to issues of discipleship today may or may not produce more martyrs (as being a Christian does not hinge on dying like Christ), but it should at least force us to question why we have been treated better than the Master, why most of us are able to escape what Jesus promised: persecution (John 15:20). I do not ask this out of a morbid desire for death or suffering. Rather, it is a truthful question about how we, as the body of Christ, are present in the world. Our very posture, as a body of people, determines how we seek the peace of the temporal city on our pilgrimage to the heavenly city.

By examining how martyrdom reveals life in communion with God, I argue that it is the apex of any true theology for the world that is mission-based. My aim, therefore, is to suggest that martyrdom is a manner of missionary work that is inescapably public and political. I opt to examine blood-witnessing as an instance of "making disciples" to stress the inherently political nature of Christianity. For the church, historically speaking, martyrdom is *the* political act because it represents the ultimate imitation of Christ, signifying a life lived in obedience to, and participation in, the triune God.[20] Martyrdom, as a doxological response to the world's rebellion against its Creator, is the liturgical culmination of a series of practices that makes possible immediate communion with the triune God. Communion cannot be private, because "communion" (like the eternal relations that constitute God's very life) depends on sociality for its intelligibility. Participation in God will therefore bear witness to who God is through the life of the participant. Such witness, if it is witness at all, will be public—it will be political.

In chapter 1 I pay close attention to early church accounts of martyrdom (up to the fourth century). I show that martyrdom, as it occurs in the early life of Christianity, is a public/political act recognized by both church and state, which suggests that any theological tendency, past or present, that depoliticizes salvation is mistaken. Furthermore, I examine how the spectacle of martyrdom is a kind of liturgical procession before the world that assumes both initiation (baptism) into the *ekklesia* and the concomitant training necessary for the second baptism. By being baptized people prepared to carry out baptism to its fullest extent, Christians offer the world an alternative to its destructiveness. In sum, I argue that the church is, inescapably, a body politic that produces a different kind of political agent, namely, the martyr.

Chapter 2 explores the body of the martyr and how the early church understood it as the site of the cosmic battle between God and those forces in rebellion against God. God battled the forces arrayed against God through God's people, and these people were victorious in the same manner in which the slaughtered Lamb was victorious. Just as the flesh of the Lamb was destroyed and resurrected, so too the martyr participated in the cosmic battle through her own skin. The flesh, for the early church, was the pivot of salvation. The body reconfigured by liturgy, specifically the Eucharist, and visibly transformed (prior to and after resurrection) was a doxological response to the privation of good within the fallen order. This chapter lays the groundwork necessary to undermine tendencies to turn Christianity, the practice of *religio*, into spirituality.[21] The way of Jesus is by no means spiritual if by spiritual one assumes a disembodied, apolitical, and privatized faith. This chapter extends the first in its attempt to remember, via the martyrs, the political nature of both salvation *and* the flesh, and the salvation *of* the flesh.

In the third chapter I look to the sixteenth century in order to examine how truthful performances of martyrdom might be located in the schisms of the reformations. Specifically, what does it mean for one ecclesial body (Catholic, Protestant, or Anabaptist) to claim martyrdom at the expense of another ecclesial body? To answer this question I will examine what constitutes politics in the sixteenth century, how this differs from the early church, and how such a shift, on certain levels, justifies the killing of Christians by other Christians. If it is possible to locate authentic performances of martyrdom in the sixteenth century, then not only may it be possible to locate truthful performances of the church (and its public witness) within the past two centuries, but this may also open the door to a better understanding of the difficulty in naming what constitutes political behavior in terms of Christian practice (indeed, it will call into question such a bifurcation).

In the fourth chapter I look to the Jeremian theme of seeking the welfare of the city as I examine what it means for Christians to live as aliens in a foreign land yet continue to seek the good of their temporal home. Following the work of the fourth-century theologian St. Augustine and the twentieth-century Mennonite theologian John Howard Yoder, I suggest, through the lineage of our martyrs, how we can faithfully seek the peace of the city. The martyrs' doxological praise—their witness—is not just intended for God; it is for the world so that it too can fulfill its divinely appointed end.

It is difficult to fathom writing an essay on witness that did not pay close attention to those who have witnessed well. For this reason I have found it important to include the stories of many of God's "fallen" throughout this book. In the final chapter I pay close attention to one particular martyr in order to give a better sense of what my argument looks like when embodied (not because a martyr embodies my argument but because his or her life/death inspires me to reflect). Thus, I examine the life and death of Archbishop Oscar Romero. I conclude with Romero simply because he died well. His life, like those of all the other martyrs mentioned throughout this book, was constituted by the habits and practices of the church in a way that made it possible for him to receive the gift of martyrdom. Romero wonderfully exemplifies what it means to seek the peace of the city, because he embodied well what it means for a Christian to engage the world. Romero chose, and was chosen for, a life of obedience that culminated in the ultimate form of *imitatio Christi*: martyrdom. Jesuit theologian Jon Sobrino calls

Romero's life "a gospel."[22] That is, Romero's life is good news inasmuch as it reveals to the world what Jesus looks like. Such news, I claim, is the most crucial kind of public and political discourse.

Finally, the epilogue refutes such language as "tragedy" and "sacrifice," because such language, as it is currently used, further depoliticizes Christianity. That these terms are so often employed in an attempt by theologians to explain things like death and suffering, whether in the case of martyrdom or not, legitimates the ontology of violence that characterizes the space and time known as the secular. Christians are privy to a different grammar—one that assumes a different world with different possibilities for action. The Christian self in this narrative, I argue, is not offered for a perpetually postponed good; rather, the offering of the self involves a return of the self. Martyrdom denies tragedy and refuses to ontologize evil by physically accepting the others' lack of good. Participation in the Eucharist creates martyrs, not victims. It positions us in the divine economy, which, while it is lived out in the temporal city, resists the categories of tragedy and sacrifice, and envisions an apocalyptic hope in the final imitation of Christ: resurrection. Resurrection is the end of sacrifice. The divine/human gift exchange, manifested by the life, death, and resurrection of Jesus (and followed by those who call him Lord), creates an apocalyptic world that ends tragedy. It is a world where the other, the martyr (as one among many "others" placed outside the walls of the territorial city), not only makes politics possible, but demonstrates true politics by witnessing to the kingdom that has arrived and is still to come.

When he opened the fifth seal, I saw under the altar the souls of those who had been slain because of the word of God and the testimony they had maintained. They called out in a loud voice, "How long Sovereign Lord, holy and true, until you judge the inhabitants of the earth and avenge our blood?" Then each of them was given a white robe, and they were told to wait a little longer, until the number of their fellow servants and brothers who were to be killed as they had been was completed.

— John of Patmos (Rev 6:9-11 NIV)

1

Spectacle: The Early Church

For I think that God has exhibited us apostles as last of all, as though sentenced to death, because we have become a spectacle to the world, to angels and to mortals.

—Paul (1 Cor 4:9)

You shall see a contest tomorrow.

—Mappalicus

Ignatius of Antioch, one of the most eccentric martyrs in Christian history (if for no other reason than his wonderfully explicit desire to imitate Christ in all things), claimed that if his body were saved from public execution, it would be difficult for him to attain God.[1] He pleaded, therefore, that his flock not attempt to rescue him from death, because such actions would not only prevent his becoming an offering to God, but were to be understood as an effort to thwart the will of God. For Ignatius, martyrs are only martyrs because they are chosen by God. If one is chosen by God to be blessed with the gift of martyrdom, one cannot and should not resist. That God elects certain Christians to imitate Christ in his death is but one way Christians are called to embody and reveal Jesus. Assuming this evangelistic account, if Ignatius's execution were to be interrupted by his well-intentioned flock, he would become but a mere voice—as opposed to a word.[2] That is, he would be but one more person who claimed to be a Christian yet had failed to seal his claims by his death. In failing to do so, it is not that Ignatius would cease to be a Christian; he simply would miss his opportunity to be, as Paul proclaims, a spectacle for the world (1 Cor 4:9). This is crucial not as a matter of pride or pathology but because as a bishop, Ignatius simply thought that the best thing he could do for his flock,

27

and for the possible conversion of non-Christians, was to seal his testimony with his life. His desire was fulfilled:

> When the whole multitude of the people were assembled, to witness the death of Ignatius (for the report had spread through the whole city, that a bishop had been brought from Syria, who, according to the sentence of the Emperor, was to fight against the wild beast), Ignatius was brought forth and placed in the middle of the amphitheatre. Thereupon Ignatius, with a bold heart, thus addressed the people which stood around: "O ye Romans, all you who have come to witness with your own eyes this combat; know ye, that this punishment has not been laid upon me on account of any misdeed or crime; for such I have in no wise committed, but that I may come to God, for whom I long, and whom to enjoy is my insatiable desire. For I am the grain of God. I am ground by the teeth of the beast, that I may be found a pure bread of Christ, who is to me the bread of life."
> . . . As soon as he had spoken these words, two dreadful, hungry lions were let out to him from their pits, who instantly tore and devoured him, leaving almost nothing, or, at least very little, even of his bones. Thus fell asleep, happy in the Lord, this faithful martyr of Jesus Christ.[3]

Known as Theophoros ("one who carries God"), Ignatius, who some church legends claim was the child whom Jesus took into his arms (Mark 9:36-37) and was also the disciple of the apostle John, imitated Christ in life, and imitated Christ in death. This was all performed under the watchful eye of the world.

Many of the elements normative for the "martyrdom" experience in the Roman arena can be found in this story: it is a victorious occasion, a public spectacle, and a liturgical act. Despite appearances, Ignatius "wins" the contest because he has so successfully followed the path of the crucified Jesus. As a public spectacle, all the world is privy to the contest between Ignatius and the beasts, rendering this a liturgical event, not just for the church but also by the state. Many martyrdoms during the first three hundred years of Christianity coincided with Roman feasts celebrating the gods or certain nobility. Perpetua and Felicitas, who will figure in the next chapter, were martyred on the birthday of Geta, the son of Septimius Severus. Ignatius was himself kept in prison until a particular feast day of the Romans (which one remains unclear) and was then brought into the theater to face death. Moreover, the games themselves often revolved around a liturgical cycle that emulated or gave praise to the gods of the Romans.[4] That many Christians were executed on birthdays of royalty, feast days, and other holidays (holy days) was no coincidence: Romans often placed executions on particular days of the year that corresponded to their own liturgical calendar. This not only speaks volumes about the Roman worldview but also says much about how the church understood, and continues to understand, the politics of martyrdom.

As the story of Ignatius reveals, martyrdom is clearly a *public* act. It does not occur in private, but is performed publicly before the masses.[5] In this sense, martyrdom is authentic public theology, not of the kind found in the last two centuries (associated with apologetics), but the kind that unapologetically reveals the world to be the world. The willingness to reveal to the world that she is the world is not only a public revelation but is also political, as martyrdom becomes the world's way of dealing with this revelation. To be executed because of one's allegiance to Christ and, hence, as an enemy of the empire, is a public/political act that captures the attention of many citizens. Such executions are political statements that governments make to their people: competing allegiances will not be tolerated. For this reason, however, the state is not alone in recognizing the political nature of martyrdom—those being martyred, as well as those naming the executed "martyrs," also recognize its political significance. Origen, for instance, assumed the political significance of martyrdom as he encouraged those approaching their death with these words:

> A great multitude is assembled to watch you when you combat and are called to martyrdom. It is as if we said that thousands upon thousands gather to watch a contest in which contestants of outstanding reputation are engaged. When you will be engaged in the conflict you can say with Paul: *We are made a spectacle to the whole world and to angels and to men.* The whole world, therefore, all the angels on the right and on the left, all men, both those on the side of God and the others—all will hear us fighting the fight for Christianity.[6]

Not just the local body politic observes this event. According to Origen, the entire cosmos views the battle between God's people and

God's enemies. Martyrdom is, therefore, the public act *par excellence*. What renders it a political act, or better, *the* political act, will be the underlying subject of this chapter.

Several areas suggest martyrdom as the apex of a faithful theological politic. First, as Paul claims in 1 Corinthians 4:9, those who follow Christ are made a spectacle to the world. Many early church documents envision martyrdom as a practice that takes place in an arena (or theater) where the entire universe is watching. This is not merely a battle between a lion and a lone second-century Christian—the fate of an empire rests on what occurs in this cosmic arena. In this sense, we discover that martyrdom is a contest not just between sinner and saint, but between a rebellious creation and God.[7]

Second, any contest assumes the necessity of training. Christians in the early church were well aware that their lives might end in martyrdom, and their liturgical practices suggest a kind of training for such an end. Early Christians never assumed that martyrdom would be an easy contest (for many fail). Rather, martyrdom required the cultivation of habits and practices that prepared the Christian for an early and violent death. These habits and practices became the training ground for a clash between disparate political bodies.

Finally, I examine how martyrdom was understood as a liturgical act that results in the recipient winning her crown. Martyrdom was viewed by many of the ante-Nicene writers as the culmination of a radically disciplined Christian life made possible by the Eucharist, baptism, and prayer—in other words, by the liturgical life of the church. Contrary to the orthodox claim that there is only one baptism, there is indeed a second baptism: the baptism of blood. This final and, ultimately, sanctifying baptism is the highest liturgical act that can be performed. It is the act by which the Christian is said to be perfected and given immediate access to heavenly communion with the triune God. Martyrdom is both a liturgical and political act, predicated on the necessity of a disciplined ecclesial life that results in a public clash with the powers-that-be. The early church's experience of martyrdom may provide us with resources necessary to wade through current debates concerning truthful political activity and faithful citizenship.

All the World's a Stage

A good moral, my lord: it is not enough to speak, but to speak true.
— Lysander in *A Midsummer Night's Dream*

In book four of *The History of the Church*, Eusebius recounts the story of Polycarp's martyrdom as a divinely orchestrated drama. The entire narrative reads as if Polycarp is merely an actor on stage, delivering the lines needed to cue the other actors into action:

> His introduction was followed by a tremendous roar as the news went round: "Polycarp has been arrested!" At length, when he stepped forward he was asked by the proconsul if he really was Polycarp. When he said yes, the proconsul urged him to deny the charge. "Respect your years!" he exclaimed, adding similar appeals regularly made on such occasions: "Swear by Caesar's fortune; change your attitude; say, 'Away with the godless!'" But Polycarp, with his face set, looked at all the crowd in the stadium and waved his hand towards them, sighed, looked up to heaven, and cried: "Away with the godless!"[8]

Polycarp's reply set "the whole mass of Smyrnaeans, Gentiles, and Jews" against him, and they immediately demanded his death. After an attempt to burn him failed, a *confector* (an official of the games whose duty was to make sure the wounded perish) was summoned to end Polycarp's life. Although the official's sword ended his earthly life, it also sealed his fate as one of the elect who received the crown of immortality.

The detailed story of Polycarp, like that of many other martyr narratives from this period, presupposes the public and political nature of executions. In the middle of a large stadium, the criminal was "introduced" to a great number of people who observed the unfolding process of trial, sentencing, and punishment. Not only did the crowd witness the narrative develop, but they also participated in it. Eusebius claimed that "the crowds rushed to collect logs and faggots" in order to prepare a fire to consume the saint.[9] Joyce E. Salisbury notes in *Perpetua's Passion* that the "crowd did not sit as simple voyeurs to the death throes of the condemned."[10] The audience participated in and interacted with the spectacle. Sometimes this played itself out in spectators wielding weapons, gathering wood for burnings, or simply demanding that someone die. All of those who constituted the audience at the theater, Rome's citizenry, were involved in the punishment of its subversives.

That the citizens of Rome participated in this public act of retribution is an essential part of being made a spectacle to the world. For in the arena, a great contest transpires. It is a contest that involves not just human observers, but also the heavenly realm. To fare well in such a contest, the third-century bishop/martyr Cyprian argues that Christians must be

> trained and prepared, and reckon it a great glory of their honour if it should happen to them to be crowned in the sight of the people, and in the presence of the emperor. Behold a lofty and great contest, glorious also with the reward of a heavenly crown, inasmuch as God looks upon us as we struggle, and extending His view over those whom He has condescended to make His sons, He enjoys the spectacle of the contest. God looks upon us in the warfare. . . . His angels look on us, and Christ looks on us.[11]

It is not just the human eye witnessing this spectacle, but the entirety of the universe gazes upon the battle—suggesting that something truly cosmic is at stake.

Throughout early Christian literature, the chief combatants in the martyrs' battle were not the Christian and the gladiator (or beast), but the battle between Christ and those powers in rebellion to Christ. This war was waged visibly in the bodies of Christians. Cyprian informs his listeners that on the day they are called to battle, they must "engage bravely, fight with constancy, as knowing that you are fighting under the eyes of a *present* Lord. . . . He Himself also wrestles in us, Himself engaged—Himself also in the struggles of our conflict not only crowns, but is crowned."[12] Tertullian contends that when Christians become martyrs, demons are defeated.[13] The arena, in effect, represents that place where the power of evil fully manifests itself in order to do battle with God.

Christians were not the only ones to assume that such a contest reflected a greater contest than that staged in the earthly realm. The Romans also imagined that what transpired in the arena mirrored judgments made by their gods. In the arena, a dangerous pagan mythos was created. The good of the Roman Empire was dependent upon what occurred in the coliseum, and it could not afford to take chances with a poor outcome.[14] In an effort to ensure an efficient theatrical event, various pagan rituals were performed that paid homage to both the gods of Rome and the emperor. Decorated in eccentric costumes, the gladiators (followed by priests, magistrates, and a whole parade of participants) entered the arena on behalf the Roman Empire. Sacrifices were made and oracles delivered.

Given that the good of the empire rested on the rituals that occurred within the space of the arena, what transpired there could not be taken for granted. It was for this reason that Tertullian forbade Christians from attending the amphitheatre. In *De Spectaculis*, or *The Shows*, he claims that an insidious religious drama, one at odds with the Christian narrative, takes place in the arena.[15] This same religious narrative demanded the worship of false gods and death to those who resisted. Citizens were either killed or exiled based on their religious convictions, and the arena often arbitrated a citizen's crime against the state. Consequently, any easy dichotomization between the political and the religious in the late ancient Roman Empire should be suspect. The arena demonstrates that religiosity cannot be separated from the political claims made and acted upon by the governing body. The religious *was* the political.

The amphitheatre (or arena) played a crucial role in the first three hundred years of Christianity, precisely because of its fundamental importance to the Roman Empire. Almost all of the cities under Roman control had an arena, and the amphitheatre in Carthage was large enough to hold about thirty thousand spectators (second in size only to the Colosseum in Rome).[16] These amphitheatres had many functions, for they "formed a central part of Roman religious sensibility, which was concerned with ritual ordering and controlling the world."[17] This intimate connection between what took place in the arena and the well-being of the Roman Empire is expressed in the proverbial saying:

> As long as the Colosseum stands, Rome shall stand;
> When the Colosseum falls, Rome will fall;
> When Rome falls, the world will fall.[18]

Given this adage, it would be difficult to overstate the importance attached to the arena in Roman politics. Indeed, the two cannot be separated. Thomas Wiedemann, commenting on this reality, argues that the arena was the "limit" of Roman civilization:

The arena was the place where civilization confronted nature, in the shape of the beasts which represented a danger to humanity, and where social justice confronted wrongdoing, in the shape of criminals who were executed there, and where the Roman empire confronted its enemies, in the persons of the captured prisoners of war who were killed or forced to kill one another in the arena.[19]

Through the games/politics of the arena, or, in other words, by means of the animals killed and enemies conquered, the Romans assured themselves that they were in control of the world.[20]

It is not difficult to imagine that Polycarp knew what was coming when he proclaimed, "Away with the atheists!" The politics of the arena could only demand one response to such disrespect: death. So, as if in a well-rehearsed drama, Polycarp was led to his death, and the harmony of the city was restored.[21]

The action taken against Polycarp was, according to Roman wisdom and authority, a morally legitimate response. Allowing such rebellion to persist would have been to allow the social fabric of the Roman world to be torn apart. Christians, therefore, were paraded into the arenas as symbols of the intolerance the state exercises toward those who refuse to sacrifice to its gods, respect its traditions and, by extension, swear allegiance to its *ordo*. That the early Christians were "paraded" into the arena was an intentional ritual used to highlight the contrasting processions that occurred within the arena. Tertullian, describing in vivid detail the procession that occurred prior to arena games and circuses, said:

The . . . ambitious preliminary display . . . to which the name procession specially belongs, is in itself the proof to whom the whole thing appertains, in the many images the long line of statues, the chariots of all sorts, the thrones, the crowns, the dresses. What high religious rites besides, what sacrifices precede, come between, and follow. How many guilds, how many priesthoods, how many offices are set astir, is known to the inhabitants of the great city in which the demon convention has its headquarters.[22]

Tertullian considers the entirety of the games to be demonically orchestrated and prohibits Christians from participating in such events (even to witness their own being slain) for fear of the demonic overcoming them.[23]

In a sense, martyrdom counters the parade of the games. In giving encouragement to Ambrose and Protoctectus, Origen recognizes the public and liturgical nature of martyrdom by advising them to go "in procession before the world."[24] Christians were led into the arena and forced to participate in games they abhorred; yet their counter-procession (one that includes both humility and pride) turned the games against the Romans. Criminals were supposed to die in fear; the crowds expected and even demanded this. Yet Christians, so to speak, had a bad habit of dying happy.[25] The young martyr Germanicus, for instance, overcame his fear of death and, in order to be with his Father in heaven all the more quickly, welcomed it. Following his death, the entire crowd was so confounded and irritated by this display of Christian heroism that they demanded the immediate deaths of the rest of the Christians in the arena.[26]

Perhaps if the early Christians had been trained to think of martyrdom as a battle fought unaided, their approach to the arena would have been different. For them, however, what transpired in the arena was not just a match between a Christian and a lion, or between a Christian and an emperor; rather, the Christian represented, that is, provided a vision of, the actual celestial battle taking place between Christ and Satan. Cyprian claimed that those who witness the Christian deaths in the arena watch "with admiration the heavenly contest—the contest of God, the spiritual contest, the battle of Christ."[27]

Here, and counter to many recent understandings of spirituality as disembodiment, the spiritual battle is a bodily battle inasmuch as it manifests itself in the body. Cyprian, for example, noted that the blood flowing from the martyr was so copious as to subdue "the flames of Gehenna with its glorious gore."[28] And, in *Church History*, Eusebius argued that Sanctus's "poor body was a witness to what he suffered—it was all wound and bruise, bent up and robbed of outward human shape, but, suffering in that body, Christ accomplished most glorious things, utterly defeating the adversary."[29]

Though the body was often viewed with suspicion in early Christianity, in the next chapter I argue that the body is not to be undermined, precisely because it is the temple of the Holy Spirit. Even Ignatius, who so ardently desired martyrdom, understood such desire to be predicated on the *humanity* of Christ. That Christ remains in his flesh after his resurrection and that in the Last Judgment we shall know him by the wounds in his flesh demands an account of the body that takes seriously the good that is the body. For Ignatius it seems crucial to reiterate the humanity of Christ against those who would deny his literal taking on of flesh.[30]

The Christology underwriting these accounts of martyrdom is in stark contrast to the heresy that is docetism. Docetists suggested that the Son of God was only divine and did not actually become flesh but merely appeared to become flesh. This early christological heresy not only denied the salvation of the flesh that Jesus' taking on of the flesh makes possible but renders nonsensical the claim that Jesus genuinely suffered in the body and will come again in the body.[31] The early church was adamant in arguing that Jesus did not appear to be human any more than humans appear to have bodies. Jesus is fully divine and fully human, and Christians are, as imitators of this God-man, embodied creatures participating in the new humanity made possible by Christ. Christianity, therefore, is no "spiritual" religion, and its substantial production of martyrs, ascetics, and virgins attests to this claim.

The heavenly/spiritual contest takes place in the flesh. Though there is a war raging in the heavenly realm, it manifests itself in the flesh and blood of each believer. This is why the incarnation is so important for Christians. That God assumes flesh renders possible the salvation of flesh, as well as the literal following of this second Adam epitomized as a slaughtered lamb. The Lamb, however, is not defeated. Despite its apparent defeat through death, death is actually defeated because the Father resurrects the Son. The very death of Jesus, his nonresistance to the powers-that-be (that, ironically, means their defeat), becomes the paradigmatic example for how followers of this God-man are to behave.

This is the way this Lamb battles and is the manner in which those who wish to follow this Lamb must battle. Martyrs perform this task well, for they wage the war of the Lamb not by resisting the empire but by submitting to it. By submitting to the authority of the empire, Christians place their faith in the authority that rules over the empire—the rule of Christ. That Christ's power took the path of the cross means that those who would be called his followers must also take this path. Yet the cross is always understood in light of the resurrection, which renders the loss of one's life as a witness, anything but tragic. This is a death that avoids the language of tragedy because it brings life as it precedes resurrection.[32] It is for this reason that martyrdom was often referred to as a "happy death."[33]

Germanicus, Polycarp, Perpetua, and the majority of Christian martyrs died happy because they died well. They died well because they understood their deaths as the end result of lives lived in obedience to Christ. Such faithful obedience, however, is not automatic, especially when it comes to the literal willingness to lose one's life in order to save it. Obedience is a skill that develops after being initiated into a communal life of holiness. In other words, obedience is learned, and it is learned by being around others who are skilled in obedience. Just as there is no Germanicus without Polycarp, so also there is no Polycarp without the church, for the church is the place where Christians learn from each other how to practice obedience. The church is the "school" that prepares Christians for the inevitable conflict that will arise when competing claims are made on their bodies. To which body politic does one belong, and how does one learn how to embody one body politic while resisting the claims of a rival body politic? That is, how do Christians prepare for the spectacle to be made of them because of their uncompromising allegiance to the ecclesia?

Basic Training: Learning How to Die Well

He [Attalus] strode in, ready for the fray, in the strength of a clear conscience, for he had trained hard in the school of Christ and had been one of our constant witnesses to the truth.

—Eusebius

It was equally clear that others were not ready, that they had not trained, and were still flabby, in no fit condition to face the strain of a struggle to the death.

—Eusebius

John Chrysostom claimed that to honor the martyrs, one must imitate them.[34] This does not mean that all Christians must become martyrs. Honoring the martyrs is not just imitating the way they died but imitating the way they lived (which is generally what led to their martyrdom). Potential martyrs realize the difficulty they face, given that the entire world opposes them. To become a Christian under the Roman Empire, at least in the first three hundred years of Christianity, entailed possible loss of goods, exile, and very often death. Christianity, therefore, was not entered into lightly. To become a Christian meant that one had to prepare for the possibility of a premature death. Such preparation went beyond the individual will of each Christian. Robin Young notes that preparations for public testimony of Christianity required "training, participation by other members of the community and their support, and a constant, intelligent grasp of the real and eschatological situation."[35]

Dying well is not a natural skill. It is not something inherent in being human. Rather, to die happy requires training in certain habits, practices, and skills that enable one to cultivate the kind of disposition for a blessed death. We should not, therefore, imagine that Eusebius, in the epigraphs above, faulted the lapsed for their poor physical appearance. Dying well in the Christian tradition has little to do with the shape of one's body. The contest that occurs between the Christian and the world, as we have seen, is a contest between Christ and Satan. What is needed is not so much physical endurance, but Christ inhabiting one's body. As Christ is unconquerable, so are those whom he inhabits.

Yet what enables one to continue to confess Christ while being tortured in unthinkable ways? Does the inhabitance of Christ in one's body through the work of the Holy Spirit make this possible? Throughout the history of the church, this has always been a central explanation for the martyrs' resolve.[36] Does this mean, however, that the martyr is immune to pain? This is doubtful: otherwise the very ability to confess Christ in light of such horrid pain would cease to be the miracle it is. The early church had its share of those unprepared for such pain (indeed, the church split over this as the controversy between the Donatists and Catholics proves) and by no means thought that the ability to endure torture was a given. To submit to torture rather than verbally disown God requires the grace of God, but it also requires a formative community that grants one the appropriate language for an authentic experience of God's grace. The church mediates God's presence because the church *is* God's presence. Those who have not looked to the church for their formation cannot be expected to persevere when their own bodies have not been properly trained by *the* body—the body of Christ.

Though training for martyrdom occurred in several ways, each according to the historical and geographical locale in which the church found itself, the most significant manner in which Christians were trained for martyrdom was through the letters of people who had previously trained for the heavenly contest. Many early Christians looked to the writings of Paul and the apostolic fathers for the proper way to give public witness. The writings of Ignatius and Polycarp, as well as the churches of Lyons and Vienne, also provide instructions for public testimony. These writings generally contain the command to imitate the faithful, to imitate Paul, and to imitate Christ. Young suggests that since "martyrs bore the name of Christ, they were themselves like letters meant to be read by the community and the world, letters from Christ that were recognizably like Christ."[37] So it was not simply a matter of reading the letters left by martyrs that constituted training, but in recognizing that the martyrs made Christ present in the world. Martyrs-in-training sensed the gravity of what was at stake and prepared themselves—via imitation of the saints—for the contest.

The Martyrdom of Polycarp was written with the clear intention to form catechumens into disciples. It claims that the Lord "shows us from above a martyrdom becoming the Gospel" in order that Christians may be clear as to what they are to imitate.[38] The details of Polycarp's martyrdom are quite similar to Jesus' own passion story: Polycarp is led into the arena under guard; he engages in a long prayer of consecration and intercession (in which is mentioned the cup of Christ and the resurrection); a voice from heaven is heard, and then he dies. The substantial similarities between Polycarp's martyrdom and Christ's passion rhetorically reinforce the following analogy: it produces the intended effect that, just as Polycarp imitates Christ, so should Christians imitate Polycarp. The imitation of Polycarp mirrors an imitation of Christ that is not supposed to short-cut direct imitation of Christ, but enables Christians to better see what imitation of Christ looks like (as interpretation is not self-evident).

It was in no way a given that a Christian would always be able to withstand the battle against her enemies. Many in the early church strayed and paid homage to Caesar in order to escape torture and punishment. The persecution of Decius, for example, found the Christians ill-prepared, and many lapsed under its weight. So, for the early Christians, preparation was considered an essential practice in the church, which, in turn, rendered the church *the* indispensable element in one's preparation for an early death.

Cyprian probably made the strongest case for the necessity of the church's practices in the life of would-be martyrs. He argued that it is in the *castra caelestia* ("camp of heaven") that one gains the tools necessary to combat the antichrist.[39] In his address to Fortunatus he stated:

> But what more fitly or more fully agrees with my own care and solicitude, than to prepare the people divinely entrusted to me, and an army established in the heavenly camp, by assiduous exhortations against the darts and weapons of the devil? For he cannot be a soldier fitted for the war who has not first been exercised in the field; nor will he who seeks to gain the crown of contest be rewarded on the racecourse, unless he first considers the use and skillfulness of his powers.[40]

In other words, the resources of the church are like field exercises in which Christians develop the skills and habits necessary to combat the "ancient adversary."

The arena was a battlefield, and just as no gladiator entered it unprepared, neither should a Christian. Christian worship was the means by which one prepared well for the contest. Prayer, charity, and the sacraments were understood to be fundamental habits that prepared one for the coming battle. Though many in the early church argued that martyrdom was a substitute for baptism, Cyprian considered it difficult for one to become a martyr unless he or she was already baptized (or at least a catechumen in preparation for baptism). If one was not baptized, one could not receive the most powerful resource of all: the Eucharist. The Eucharist, Cyprian argued, serves as protection for the recipient; it strengthens the Christian with the blood and body of Christ. Christians cannot lack this protection, nor is it possible for Christians to shed their own blood unless they participate in the sharing of blood that Christ shed for all.[41]

To be a martyr, or to be named a martyr, implies the tacit recognition, as we shall see in chapter 3, of the embodiment of true doctrine. In this sense, martyrs are "not only trained and created by teaching; they are . . . guarantors of true teaching."[42] There can be no separation between doctrine and ethics in the lives of the martyrs. That is, there is no dualism between teaching and living, theory and practice, the discursive and the nondiscursive. To both live and die well requires seeing and understanding the world well.

In Christianity, that vision created by such a "seeing" is constituted by faithful doctrine. The martyrs are martyrs because their deaths (and lives) reflect orthodox teaching. Irenaeus speaks at length on this subject and even claims that the result of the genuine teaching of the church is its own persecution:

> For the Church *alone* sustains with purity the reproach of those who suffer persecution for the righteousness' sake, and endure all sorts of punishments, and are put to death because of the love which they bear to God, and their confession of His Son . . . similar to that of the ancient prophets . . . the Lord declares, "For so persecuted they the prophets who were before you," inasmuch as she does indeed, in a new fashion, suffer persecution from those who do not receive the word of God, while the self-same spirit rests upon her [as upon these ancient prophets].[43]

In continuity with the prophets, the church continues to be persecuted for its adherence to the true God. Those who claim that such persecution is unnecessary are not of the church and stand in discontinuity with the story of Israel. For Irenaeus, the bodily witness of the church is the sign of its authenticity.[44] The embodiment of Christian faith is made possible by right doctrine, baptism, Eucharist, worship, and prayer—all of which constitute the possibility of producing martyrs.

Martyrdom itself becomes something of a sacrament insofar as it becomes a skilled practice intelligible only in light of other practices in the church. Commenting on Irenaeus's account of persecution and the Eucharist, Young argues that "Christ's sacrificed flesh renews the flesh of those who have inherited the promise, and these are preeminently the martyrs." She continues by suggesting that martyrdom is "valued by the Christian community itself as a spectacle and a display of the eventual triumph of God's elect. It has certain ceremonial aspects for which people train, aspects that reflect baptism and the Eucharist."[45] Martyrdom is not only a public act; it is a public liturgy.

A Second (Orthodox) Baptism

If the Eucharist of the early Christians was a kind of substitutive sacrifice, then the martyrs' was an imitative one. When the Eucharist was still private, not open to non-Christian view, the martyrs' sacrifice was public and dramatic.

—Robin Darling Young

The act of martyrdom, the naming of which is the church's ability to call a Christian's death a witness to Jesus, takes on its own liturgical significance. Martyrdom is sacramental because it is a second baptism. This is not a rebaptism, for this second baptism is of a wholly different nature than the first. Yet, as seen with Cyprian, the second baptism is unintelligible without the first.

Martyrdom is inseparable from baptism and the Eucharist, and like these two sacraments, it too is a ritual. Young argues that in all likelihood it was "imagined ahead of time and understood as both a repetition of baptism or a substitute for it, and a sacrifice parallel and similar to Christ's passion and the Eucharist, that is to say, a redemptive sacrifice."[46] Although martyrdom was often understood as a substitute for baptism (as in the work of Cyril of Jerusalem), it did not undermine baptism. It was only understood as a substitute, strictly speaking, if the one martyred had not yet been baptized (as in the case, for example, of a catechumen). Martyrdom was recognized, however, as the second and loftier baptism—one that truly eradicated sin.

Cyprian argued that those who have received the first baptism should also prepare for the second baptism. He said that the second baptism is

> greater in grace, more lofty in power, more precious in honor—
> a baptism wherein angels baptize—a baptism in which God and
> His Christ exult—a baptism after which no one sins any more—
> a baptism which completes the increase of our faith—a baptism
> which . . . immediately associates us with God.[47]

Cyprian is suggesting that through the baptism of water, the *remission* of one's sins occurs, but through the baptism of blood the *end* of one's sins occurs. The end of sin was made possible through the gift of martyrdom. Martyrdom was a graced medicine given to the elect as a gift from God.[48] The second baptism was a thing to be "embraced and desired, and to be asked for in all the entreaties of our petitions, that we who are God's servants should also be his friends."[49]

Origen also wrote on the baptism of blood and, in words quite similar to Cyprian's, stated:

> Let us remember also the sins that we have committed, and that except by baptism it is not possible to obtain remission of sins. But according to the laws of the Gospel one cannot be baptized twice in water and the spirit for the remission of sins. We are given, however, the baptism of martyrdom.[50]

Origen's theology of martyrdom derived from Jesus' question, "Are you able to drink the cup that I drink, or to be baptized with the baptism with which I am baptized?"[51] If Christians are to be true imitators of Christ, they too must be willing to drink of the cup that Jesus drinks. The "chalice of salvation," as Origen called it, is *the* term for martyrdom. Those who drink from this chalice will "sit, reign, and judge beside the King of Kings."[52] The martyrs, due to their participation in the baptism of blood, are not judged by God, but judge with God.[53]

Tertullian devoted a few comments to the second baptism in which he argued that Christians do have a "second font" that is inseparable from the first.[54] Since Christ had already been baptized by water and yet claimed to have to undergo another baptism, the second time by blood, Christians must recognize the necessity of two baptisms. Tertullian claimed that Christians are redeemed by these two baptisms. He claimed that the "uncleanness, indeed, is washed away by baptism, but the stains are changed into dazzling whiteness by martyrdom."[55] As 1 John 5:6 indicates, Jesus came by means of water and blood in order "to make us, in like manner, *called* by *water*, *chosen* by *blood*."[56] Tertullian argued that from Jesus' pierced wounds flow both water and blood, so that we might be bathed by water and nourished by blood.[57]

To be nourished by Christ's blood, however, Christians must be willing to shed their own blood. Reflecting on Revelation 17, Tertullian wrote, "When great Babylon . . . is represented as drunk with the blood of the saints, doubtless the supplies needful for drunkenness are furnished by the cups of martyrdoms."[58] In *The Passion of Perpetua and Felicitas*, a writing generally attributed to Tertullian, Saturus was thrown to a leopard and "bathed with such a quantity of blood, that the people shouted out to him as he was returning, the testimony of his second baptism, 'Saved and washed, saved and washed.'" Tertullian concluded that Saturus "was assuredly saved" given his glorification in the cosmic spectacle.[59]

Tertullian was more demanding than many of the other ante-Nicene theologians in that he assumed all Christians owe a blood-witness to God. All believers "are under the obligation to suffer martyrdom."[60] Yet owing a blood-witness and having to perform it are two different things. Tertullian insisted that martyrdom is not for everyone. Martyrdom is only for those who have been chosen by God to participate in the second baptism. In the Gospel of Matthew, Jesus proclaims, "Blessed are those who are persecuted for righteousness' sake, for theirs is the kingdom of heaven" (5:10). To suffer persecution signals one's election by God. To be a martyr is to be one of the elect.[61] Consequently, martyrdom is neither a misfortune nor a tragedy, but a gift from God "and unquestionable proof" of fidelity to God.[62] It enables one to complete one's journey of being a Christian.

In strikingly similar language, Ignatius claimed that his discipleship does not even begin until he is on his way to the arena (this allows us to make sense of Ignatius's claim that he may be called a Christian, and deemed a faithful one, when he no longer exists in the world).[63] It is not a pathological desire to pray for martyrdom, but a rightly ordered desire that finds completion in the ultimate imitation of Christ. Martyrdom renders one a participant in the divine economy and ensures one of his or her place in eternal communion with the triune God. Cyprian claimed:

> Every perfection and condition of life is included in martyrdom. This is the foundation of life and faith, this is the safeguard of salvation, this is the bond of liberty and honor; and although there are other means whereby the light may be attained, yet we more easily arrive at nearness to the promised reward, by help of these punishments that sustain us. . . . What, then, is martyrdom? It is the end of sins, the limits of dangers, the guide of salvation, the teacher of patience, the home of life, on the journey to which those things moreover befall which in the coming crisis might be considered torments.[64]

Through martyrdom the Christian is perfected; martyrdom is *the* sanctifying act.[65]

The Purple Crown

The martyr is sanctified, and through martyrdom, friendship with God is consummated as one's place in the kingdom of heaven is guaranteed. Chrysostom calls this movement of the martyr to God an "emigration into heaven."[66] For all the aforementioned theologians, martyrdom ensures one a place in heaven. For Tertullian, this assurance is immediate. He claimed that "no one, on becoming absent from the body, is at once a dweller in the presence of the Lord, except by the prerogative of martyrdom."[67] In his *Treatise on the Soul*, Tertullian was even more explicit:

> How is it . . . that the region of Paradise, which as revealed to John in the Spirit lay under the altar, displays no other souls as in it besides the souls of the martyrs? How is it that the most heroic martyr Perpetua on the day of her passion saw only her fellow-martyrs there, in the revelation which she received of Paradise. . . ? Observe, then, the difference between a heathen and a Christian in their death: if you have to lay down your life for God, as the Comforter counsels, it is not in gentle fervors and soft beds, but in the sharp pains of martyrdom: you must take up the cross and bear it after the Master, as He has Himself instructed you. *The sole key to unlock Paradise is your own life's blood.*[68]

Cyprian, in agreement with Tertullian, quoted Psalm 116:15: "Precious in the sight of the LORD is the death of his saints" (NIV), and then added, "Precious is the death which has bought immortality at the cost of its blood, which has received the crown from the consummation of its virtues."[69] Though the "pain" of death is real—it is no easy death— the reward is great. Cyprian claimed that martyrs will receive more in reward for their suffering than what they suffer in the passion itself. Following the parable of the sower in Matthew 13, Cyprian argued that the martyrs are like the seed that falls on the ground and brings forth fruit a hundredfold—their reward shall likewise be a hundredfold.[70]

The martyr is not the only one to benefit from her imitation of Christ. Martyrdom proves to be more efficacious for those "left behind" than if the martyr had been allowed to live. Hence Tertullian's famous proclamation that the blood of the martyrs is the seed of the church.[71] The more Christians are "mowed down," the more their numbers grow. Cyprian, remarking on the glory of the church, claimed that she is purified through the blood of her own:

> She was white before in the works of the brethren; now she has become purple in the blood of the martyrs. Among her flowers are wanting neither roses nor lilies. Now let each one strive for the largest dignity of either honor. Let them receive crowns, either white, as of labours, or of purple, as of suffering. In the heavenly camp both peace and strife have their own flowers, with which the soldier of Christ may be crowned for glory.[72]

For Cyprian, the crown is purple because it reflects the blood spilled and bruises gained to receive it. The purple crown forever displays the cost, and joy, of discipleship.

For Tertullian, the notion of the purple crown assumed even more significance. In his work *On Idolatry*, he forbade Christians to wear the color of purple because it signifies royalty.[73] He also demanded in *The Chaplet* that Christians avoid wearing crowns, for they too symbolize the pomp, base glories, and false honor of the secular world.[74] Yet when Christians become martyrs, they are awarded crowns (gold for Clement of Alexandria, purple for Cyprian, white for Tertullian), suggesting that true royalty and true politics stem from obedience to Christ, not obedience to earthly powers. This is no more clearly evident than in the anecdote with which Tertullian began *De Corona*:

> Very lately it happened thus: while the bounty of our most excellent emperors were dispensed in the camp, the soldiers, laurel-crowned, were approaching. One of them, more a soldier of God, more steadfast than the rest of his brethren, who had imagined that they could serve two masters, his head alone uncovered, the useless crown in his hand—already even by that peculiarity known to everyone as a Christian—was nobly conspicuous. Accordingly, all began to mark him out, jeering him at a distance, gnashing on him near at hand. The murmur is wafted to the tribune, when the person had just left the ranks. The tribune at once put the question to him, "Why are you so different in your attire?" He declared that he had no liberty to wear the crown with the rest. Being urgently asked for his reasons, he answered, "I am a Christian." O soldier! Boasting thyself in God. Then the

case was considered and voted on; the matter was remitted to a higher tribunal; the offender was conducted to the prefects. At once he put away the heavy cloak, his disburdening commenced; he loosed from his foot the military shoe, beginning to stand upon holy ground; he gave up the sword, which was not necessary either for the protection of our Lord; from his hand likewise dropped the laurel crown; and now, purple-clad with the hope of his own blood . . . crowned more worthily with the white crown of martyrdom.[75]

Though for Tertullian the crown is white (to contrast the purple-clad colors that must be shed to receive it), it still suggests that martyrdom is understood by the church as an explicitly political act. No less political, the ante-Nicene Fathers would have argued, are the lives lived that lead to martyrdom.

In this chapter I have attempted to lay out a theology of martyrdom as understood in the early church in order to disclose how martyrdom, as a specific act within a larger vocation of witnessing, imitates the one who suffered death under Pontius Pilate. That the early church understood martyrdom to be deserving of a purple crown reveals much about the political sensibilities of the early Christians and how we, almost two millennia later, can begin to think about what it means to be a Christian under the constant duress of domesticating our faith in order to be politically relevant. What seems to be most under attack, I contend, is the body of the Christian. For this reason, in the next chapter I will examine how the body, in light of martyrdom, was understood during the "golden age" of martyrdom.

2

Body: The Field of Combat

You can kill us, but you cannot hurt us.

—Justin Martyr

Caro est cardo salutis.

—Tertullian

On March 7, 202 CE, under the rule of Septimius Severus, a small group of Christians was executed in an arena in Carthage. Of the six or so executed, two martyrs stand out in particular: Perpetua and Felicitas. The chronicle of their martyrdoms has been widely popular throughout the history of Christianity. In the early North African church, the story of these two young female martyrs was so popular that Augustine actually complained that their narrative was more widely read than Scripture.[1]

Perhaps the popularity of their account can be attributed to its narration: it was partially told by Perpetua herself. Her account is remarkably descriptive and personal, which strips it of certain problems inherent in later hagiography. In her story we do not simply encounter unblemished martyrs, as if they merely represent unreal people who, almost magically, bear witness to Christ through their blood. Rather, we collide with an account of flesh-and-blood women whose bodies are vividly described in order to make real the drama that takes place within the Roman arena.

Because the act of martyrdom is a politico-physical act (politics and bodies being inseparable), the means of execution and torture are performed for the entire world to see. Execution must take the form of a spectacle to ensure that those watching continue to structure their bodily practices in line with the desires of the empire. Consequently, the martyrdom narrative highlights the spectacle of Felicitas and Perpetua's march to the arena:

The day of their victory dawned, and the martyrs went from the prison to the amphitheatre as if they were on their way to heaven. Their faces were radiant; they were beautiful. They were moved, not by fear but by joy. Perpetua followed at a gentle pace, as a great lady of Christ, as the darling of God; the power of her gaze forced the spectators to lower their eyes. Felicitas followed her, rejoicing that she had given birth in safety so that she might fight the beasts, from blood to blood, from midwife to gladiator, to find in her second baptism her purification from childbirth.

The story of the two "beautiful" martyrs grows even more vivid in detail:

After being stripped and enclosed in nets they were brought into the arena. The people were horrified, seeing that one was a tender girl, the other a woman fresh from childbirth, with milk dripping from her breasts. . . . Perpetua was tossed first and fell on her loins. As soon as she could sit up, she noticed her tunic was torn at the side; immediately she pulled it together to cover her thighs, more mindful of her modesty than of her suffering. Then she looked for a pin and fastened her disordered hair. For it was not seemly for a martyr to suffer with her hair disheveled, lest she should seem to mourn in the hour of her glory.[2]

Felicitas's breasts leak milk, and Perpetua protects her modesty via a tunic and a hairpin. The great cosmic battle, the one that will be the "day of their victory," occurred through the vulnerability of the flesh.

Early Christian accounts of the body are often lurid and shocking to modern sensibilities. Such accounts present a world full of pain, suffering, and death. At the same time, precisely because of the inescapability of such a world, early Christian writers also present images of the body as well trained and disciplined (or at least in need of training and disciplining). The body must subject itself to ascetic practices to prepare itself for inevitable pain and suffering. As we saw in chapter 1, Eusebius stated that many Christians were incapable of martyrdom because they had "not trained," and were "still flabby, in no fit condition to face the strain of a struggle to the death."[3] One of the pragmatic reasons why the early church opposed voluntary martyrdoms was for fear of failure. Martyrdom is a skill that must be cultivated; therefore, there is no guarantee of success in one's death witness. Failure was seen as detrimental to the church because if the would-be martyr recanted, victory went to the gods of the empire. Therefore the church adamantly opposed those who sought their death for various theological reasons, but also because the church understood that martyrdom does not occur for just anyone. Those who are fortunate to receive the gift of martyrdom do so because they have reconfigured their bodies according to the liturgy and "do not find it hard to die for the true God."[4]

As stated in chapter 1, the body is the field of contestation between God and Satan. The battle between God and Satan over the realm of all creation manifests itself in the bodies of creation. This means that the body is the site of the heavenly *agon*. The contest between God and those forces opposed to God are waged in the flesh and bones of God's people. The body is not only the privileged site by which participation in the divine economy occurs, it is also the site where the battle for the cosmos takes place.

Because the battle manifests itself in the flesh of Christ's disciples, the flesh gains a privileged place in soteriology. Though the flesh is often understood in Scripture and Christian theology to be an obstacle to the right ordering of the will, it is also posited to be the very condition on which salvation hinges. That is, human flesh, fully realized in Jesus, is the site where salvation occurs. Since God becomes human in order to save humanity, there is a certain salvific contingency attached to the flesh. If God does not take on flesh or if God merely appears to take on flesh, then flesh cannot be redeemed. For Tertullian, this meant that the body is the "pivot" of salvation. In his defense of the goodness of the flesh, he stated that there is

> not a soul that can at all procure salvation, except it believe whilst it is in the flesh, so true is it that the flesh is the very condition on which salvation hinges. And since the soul is, in consequence of its salvation, chosen to the service of God, it is the flesh which actually renders it capable of such service.[5]

The body matters because we are created to live as doxological embodiments of the goodness of God.

In this chapter, I will examine how the early church attempted to reconfigure the body to better perform its doxological role. The shaping of the body by liturgical formation and the witnessing of Christ through martyrdom are part of what it means to simultaneously praise God and reveal to the world who God is. I will examine briefly the account of Polycarp's martyrdom to see how his own body, as the site of the heavenly contest, functioned as a doxological witness. Finally, I will argue that the body, as a doxological witness, returns to the earth only to complete its imitation of Christ by means of resurrection.

Doxological Bodies

Cyprian claimed that those who are privy to the martyrdoms in the pagan arena watch "with admiration the heavenly contest—the contest of God, the spiritual contest, the battle of Christ."[6] The language of a "spiritual" contest must be heard carefully. Contemporary popular culture can speak of faith as if it belongs to a disembodied realm. To be religious is to be spiritual and to be spiritual is to transcend the need for bodily disciplining. Today God is often experienced on a one-on-one basis, thus limiting the need to discipline, shape, and train one's body by the church's liturgy. God is participated in, or at least "experienced," without need of any mediating social body or practices.[7]

Spirituality within the early church, however, was hardly disembodied. The spiritual battle was a material battle and, as such, a battle that occurred in the body. Cyprian mentioned in graphic detail that the blood that flows from the martyrs subdues "the flames of Gehenna with its glorious gore."[8] Tertullian noted that the pagan crowds were painfully aware of the "delicate frame" of Perpetua and the breasts of Felicitas that were "still dropping from her recent childbirth."[9] Eusebius told us that Sanctus's "poor body was a witness to what he suffered—it was all wound and bruise, bent up and robbed of outward human shape."[10] For these Christians, the battle they waged was truly a spiritual battle, but it was also a spiritual battle waged visibly in the body. Eusebius continued by noting that, despite Sanctus's abused body, "Christ accomplished most glorious things, utterly defeating the adversary."[11]

In summary, one might say that the spiritual battle waged by Christ is waged through the body of his followers and is dependent on Christ's taking of human form and waging the same battle in his own flesh. It seems right, moreover, to suggest that in the early church the body was spiritual only inasmuch as the humanity of Jesus was material. Jesus does not "appear" to be human (contra Docetism) any more than humans appear to have, or be, bodies. Consequently, it is because Jesus is fully human (and fully divine) that martyrdom is at all intelligible. The incarnation of God in Jesus of Nazareth demands that we imitate what it means to be fully human because Jesus is the human who redefines what it means to be human. Christians are embodied creatures living into their new understanding of what it means to be human (by being a new creature in Christ), and Christianity's substantial production of ascetics, virgins, and martyrs denies any kind of spirituality that would promote disembodiment.

Elaine Scarry argues that between the Old and New Testaments a materialistic shift occurs in scriptural accounts of the body because in the latter testament God assumes human form.[12] In the Old Testament, God is without a body and whatever "it" is of God that can be "seen" leads to instant death (save for Moses, who is allowed to see God's "back" or "aftermath" in Ex 34:33). This does not mean that the body is unimportant in the Old Testament, for "it is in the body that God's presence is recorded."[13] To allow one's own body to become a vessel for the divine, whether to speak prophecy, judgment, or blessings, suggests that intimacy with God, as well as the substantiation of God, occurs within the body. Scarry is clearly not suggesting that the Old Testament is without a rich account of the body, for disobedience to God is habitually described in Scripture as a "withholding" of the body.[14] She does, however, note the vital shift that occurs between a bodiless God and God's manifestation of God's self in Jesus of Nazareth.

Though Christian orthodoxy affirms that the triune God is bodiless, it also affirms that the second person of the Trinity is a Jew named Jesus.[15] God can now be "viewed," and Christians are to embody a life that witnesses to the once-visible manifestation of God in Jesus.

Good vision, or the ability to see things well, is crucial to Christian practice and is predicated on how the New Testament highlights the importance of the sight of God and God's miracles. The Gospel of John not only invites its readers to "come and see" (1:39, 46) what good thing has come from Nazareth, but invites us to witness the "greater things" that will occur because the Son of God has come to earth (1:51). John the Baptist himself came not as the light but as a witness to the light that comes "walking toward him" (John 1:8, 29).

The New Testament, Scarry writes, is the "story of the sentient body of God being seen and touched by the sentient body of man."[16] In the New Testament, as in the Old, the human body still substantiates the existence of God, but it does so by the "bodily alteration of sensory apprehension."[17] The Gospel of Matthew states:

> And great multitudes came to Him. Bringing with them those who were lame, crippled, blind, dumb, and many others, and they laid them down at His feet; and He healed them, so that the multitude marveled as they saw the dumb speaking, the crippled restored, and the lame walking, and the blind seeing; and they glorified the God of Israel. (15:30-31 NAS)

It is the thousands who gather on the beach to watch and hear Jesus preach, the woman who merely touches Jesus' garment and is immediately healed, and the blind man who is cured by the mixture of dirt and Jesus' spit that verify, in an extraordinarily physical manner, the existence of God.

The possibility for the verification of the existence of God, or what Stanley Hauerwas calls "our only argument for the existence of God," is Christian witness.[18] The particular embodiment such witness requires is predicated on specific bodily practices. Discipleship itself entails, as the root suggests, discipline. If Christianity is to avoid disembodiment (which would produce the possible disappearance of Christianity), our bodies must come under some measure of disciplining. The various forms of ascetic practices that thrived in the fourth and fifth centuries of Christianity attest to the attempt to reshape the body according to the likeness of Christ. Scarry argues against those who assume that the "self-flagellation" of the Christian ascetic is an act of denying the body. Rather, she claims that it is a "way of so emphasizing the body that the contents of the world are cancelled and the path is clear for the entry of an unworldly, contentless force."[19]

Though it may be difficult to understand how certain practices of the desert ascetics are supposed to enable them to be better disciples, it is significant to note that many of their biographers often refer to their bodies as "heavenly" or "angelic." Many pilgrims who visited these ascetics, we are told, imagined that they were glimpsing a foretaste of the heavenly body.[20] What is important about these ascetics is not whether they actually provide a glimpse of angelic bodies, but that they understood that if they were to live continuously in the presence of God, their very own materiality required transformation.[21]

In the case of the martyrs, bodily transformation is necessary if they are to witness effectively to those around them. By withstanding persecution and torture, the martyr's body transcends normal human limitations and becomes a witness to the reality of God.[22] Such a witness, however, is impossible if the body has not already been subjected to liturgical formation. If the body is the site at which power is contested, it will require training and disciplining to resist certain counter-forms of power (the "principalities and powers") inscribing their narratives on the body.[23] The body must undergo a transformation that will enable it to perform its "world" as well as resist other worlds attempting to form it.

Immersion in liturgical practices, I argue, is the key to the kind of bodily transformation necessary for Christian performance. This transformation makes it possible not only to endure the horrors of the arena (that is, to perform well), but also to resist the powers of this world (Eph 6:12) from placing its own meta-inscription on the body of the Christian. The disciplined flesh of the martyr, though it participates (willingly or not) in the continual making and remaking of the world that occurs in the Roman arena, partakes in the world to come by its participation in the heavenly banquet. Thus it presents an image of the body that represents a new self, a new body, and a new society.[24] The body becomes the locus by which a world, one that is at odds with the world of the arena, is created. Such a world, however, is dependent on the remaking of the body. This remaking of the world/body requires, for the Christian, engagement with the church's liturgy.

Therese Lysaught argues that if Christian bodies are to display Christian claims, they will need to be shaped by Christian practices.[25] The specific practices, rituals, and habits that constitute Christianity (including, but not limited to, prayer, hymn singing, baptism, Eucharist, works of mercy) shape and form the Christian body. For example, by praying, Christians take on new postures, literally, that aid in the creation of an open and vulnerable body toward God and others. By singing, Christians vocalize their praise that makes known the Christian's allegiance. This allegiance, a new creation made possible by the revolutionary act of baptism, realigns our bodies away from the false idols of the market, state, or family, and direct us toward God.

The works of mercy, that is the feeding of the homeless, the visiting of those in prison, the providing of shelter for those without, demand that our bodies enact the very lifestyle of Jesus. We are literally redirected from a myriad forms of life to one in particular, that of discipleship.[26] As Christians we engage in and are engaged by these practices and, as a result, are formed in a way not possible without them. Lysaught claims that both the body of Christ (the church) and the bodies belonging to the body of Christ (the individual members or "limbs") are called to perform and enact Christ in the world. Our bodies are to be both doxological performances of God's good creation and resistance to those powers that attempt to subvert and otherwise determine God's creation.

Discipleship, as a mode of performance and, secondarily, resistance, is a mark of the church rooted in the Eucharist.[27] According to Lysaught, the practice of the Eucharist may be the most determinative practice of the church because it makes the church possible.[28] If there is no broken body and no spilled blood of Christ, it is difficult to imagine that there could be a church, for it is the body of Jesus that makes the body of Christ, the church, possible. Thus it seems to follow that only by the feeding on his body can the body of the Christian be made possible. If this is the case, it can be said that the consumption of the Eucharist creates within us an ontological change. By feeding on the body of Christ, we are transformed into a different creature, one that remembers the sacrifice of Christ and now pledges to participate in that soteriological reality known as the kingdom of God. Our bodies are reconfigured, because they are now directed toward the redemption and reconciliation that Jesus made possible through the cross.

Quite often, as in the experience of the early church, partaking of the flesh and blood of Christ generates other effects. For the martyrs, the Eucharist (and the concomitant training that participation in the Eucharist assumes—catechesis, repentance, and baptism) produces bodies capable of resisting imperial torture. In *Torture and Eucharist*, William T. Cavanaugh stresses the intimate connection between the martyrs and the Eucharist in the early church. He argues that many martyrs regarded the Eucharist as the essential preparation for the coming persecution. He notes that under the persecution of Diocletian "the martyrs of Abitinae adopted the motto *sine dominico non possumus*, for they would have seen the Eucharist as an invitation to, and the beginnings of, the heavenly banquet of which they were about to partake in full."[29]

By feeding on the flesh and blood of Christ, martyrs are capable of having their own flesh and blood broken in service of God. This does not suggest that the consumption of the elements produces a supernatural numbness to torture or apathy toward death (though, in many cases, Christ's dwelling in the bodies of the martyrs seems to negate the pain); rather, the disciplining of the body that occurs prior to admittance to the table, the consistent regime of practices that constitutes an ascetic life (prayer, the chanting of psalms, fasting, manual labor, and so on) and, finally, the sustained discipline of regular participation in the Eucharist over an entire lifetime is what makes imitation of Christ possible.[30]

Maureen Tilley suggests that asceticism, which depends on the liturgy, is the primary defense of the martyrs.[31] She argues against the prevalent narrative that assumes asceticism developed after the church no longer faced the immediate threat of persecution (from the fourth to fifth centuries on). Asceticism, she proposes, is the *prerequisite* for martyrdom. It stems from the Greek term *askesis*, indicating athletic training, exercise, and discipline with the intention of improving bodily performance.[32] Tilley claims that asceticism, or the conditioning of the body, is what makes it possible for martyrs to withstand crippling and ultimately fatal torture.

The conditioning of the body relies on the church body for its "production." While individual martyrs have to face the struggle of torture and slow death in their own skins, it is not clear that they could do so if their bodies lacked the training necessary to prepare for such an event. Again, the church trains its member for the heavenly contest. Such training includes prayers, hymn singing, exhortations from clergy, visitations from fellow Christians, and the witness of other martyrs. The reconfiguration the Eucharist exercises on the individual body does so only in the peculiar body politic known as the church.

In elevating the flesh as a graced means by which we become partakers in the divine (2 Pet 1:4), no argument/body can usurp the authority of the martyrs. The martyrs embody what it means to be beatified through the elective grace of God. Their lives and deaths fulfill the command to glorify God with their flesh (1 Cor 6:20), proving worthy of the dwelling of the Holy Spirit (6:19).

No Bones About It: The Body of Polycarp

The famous account of the bishop Polycarp's martyrdom accentuates an interesting connection between bodily witness and liturgical formation: the body, because it engages in formative practices, becomes a doxological response to the paganism of the hostile arena. Polycarp's witness, so the story tells us, is not so much predicated on his words as it is on his body.

When the proconsul offered Polycarp the opportunity to evangelize the crowd Polycarp said, "I would have counted you worthy to be reasoned with; for we have been taught to give honor as it is fit, where we can without harm, to governments and powers ordained by God, but I do not think the people worthy to hear any defense from me."[33] Nevertheless, the audience heard (and saw and smelled) the message:

> Those who were appointed for the purpose kindled the fire. And as the flame blazed forth in great fury, we, to whom it was given to witness it, beheld a great miracle. . . . For the fire, shaping itself in the form of an arch, like the sail of a ship when filled with the wind, encompassed as by a circle the body of the martyr. And he appeared within not like flesh which is burnt, but as bread that is baked, or as gold and silver glowing in a furnace. Moreover, we perceived such a sweet odour (coming from the pile), as if frankincense or some such precious spices had been smoking there.
>
> At length, when those wicked men perceived that his body could not be consumed by the fire, they commanded an executioner to go near and pierce him through with a dagger. And on his doing this, there came forth a dove, and a great quantity of blood, so that the fire was extinguished; and all the people wondered that there should be a difference between the unbelievers and the elect.[34]

The large crowds were struck by the difficulty of killing the eighty-six-year-old bishop and "wondered that there should be such a difference" between the dying of the unbelievers and the elect. What appears to have marveled the audience was that Polycarp's body behaved like no body they had ever witnessed. His life, as aged as it was, was difficult to end. His flesh baked rather than burned. When he was stabbed by a dagger, his blood quenched the flames surrounding his body. The body of this supposed atheist awed the crowd because it reacted to execution in a manner betraying a different formation. Even his eventual death displayed a peace (the dove flying out of his side) absent in pagan death. What the spectators witnessed, we can infer, was nothing short of Polycarp's union with God.

Lysaught writes that the "nature of Polycarp's death turns us to the question of bodily reconfiguration and how the text reads this transformation liturgically."[35] His death, which is supposed to occur through fire, does not go as planned. Despite being subjected to the torture of fire, his "ascetic and liturgical reconfiguration" enables his body to withstand the flames only to be later killed by a dagger.[36] This liturgical reconfiguration is hardly subtle in the account of Polycarp's death. After being bound, he looked to heaven and prayed,

> O Lord God Almighty, the Father of thy beloved and blessed son Jesus Christ, by whom we have received the knowledge of Thee, the God of angels and powers, and of every creature, and of the whole race of the righteous who live before thee, I give Thee thanks that Thou hast counted me worthy of this day and hour, that I should have part in the number of thy martyrs, in the cup of thy Christ, to the resurrection of eternal life, both of soul and body, through the incorruption of the Holy Ghost. . . . I praise Thee for all things, I bless Thee, I glorify Thee, along with the everlasting and heavenly Jesus Christ, Thy beloved Son, with whom, to Thee, and the Holy Ghost, be glory both now and to all coming ages. Amen.[37]

The liturgical motifs of prayer and the Eucharist are central to both the life and the death of Polycarp. The bishop continually prayed throughout his ordeal and did so with, as Lysaught notes, the formidable ease of long practice: "Trained in prayer, the words come easy. Practiced in the Eucharist, Polycarp has himself become the Eucharistic offering, the bread and the wine. He has become incorporated into Christ."[38] The fire did not end his life, for his "holy flesh" was impervious to its objective.[39] The author of the *Martyrdom of Polycarp* described his flesh as one smelling of sweet perfume. It did not even burn. Rather, his flesh appeared to bake like bread in an oven.

The death of Polycarp completed his discipleship. There is no further point, in this life, by which he can imitate Christ. However, his witness continues beyond death. The martyr's witness is not limited to life, for the body of the martyr experiences "one final transformation which continues their practice of discipleship: the dead bodies are transformed into relics."[40]

The *Martyrdom of Polycarp* represents one of the earliest accounts of the preservation of relics in church history. After an executioner completed Polycarp's martyrdom, the surrounding Christians were eager to collect his body but were denied by the "adversary of the race of the righteous" who

> perceived the impressive nature of his martyrdom, and [considered] the blameless life he had led from the beginning, and how he was not crowned with the wreath of immortality, having beyond dispute received his reward, he did his utmost that not the least memorial of him should be taken away by us, although man desired to do this, and to become possessors of his holy flesh. . . . The centurion . . . placed the body in the midst of the fire, and consumed it. Accordingly, we afterwards took up his bones, as being more precious than the most exquisite jewels, and more purified than gold, and deposited them in a fitting place, whither, being gathered together, as opportunity is allowed us, with joy and rejoicing, the Lord shall grant us to celebrate the anniversary of his martyrdom, both in memory of those who have already finished their course, and for the exercising and preparation of those yet to walk in their steps.[41]

The body of Polycarp was significant not only in life, for in death his body continued to witness to Christ. Just as he assembled Christians together for the celebration of Eucharist countless times throughout his clerical career, after his martyrdom he still brought them together as they gathered to consume the elements over his own remains. The body of Christ gathered to remember Polycarp on the anniversary of his martyrdom (his "birthday," as it is often called) solely for the purpose of worship and praise of the triune God.

Polycarp's ability to resist demands to recant his faith was due to his extensive training and his feeding on the body of Christ. This is not simply the ability to endure torture (though it is this too) but it is the ability to bear, as Ignatius claimed, the attacks of the prince of this world.[42] Like a "noble athlete" who suffers wounds and yet prevails, so too will the Christian gain victory through enduring the attacks of the evil one.[43] These attacks are endured not as ends in themselves but because they give glory to God, who in return resurrects the body of the martyr. Death, for the Christian, does not indicate the end of bodily existence; rather, it is but a mere interruption in its existence that provides the necessary route to complete union with God.

Post-resurrection embodiment became a very important theological motif in the early church. When the smoke cleared, all that was left of Polycarp's body, the supposed victor, was ashes. In this context, one could debate whether the empire or the church had prevailed. Both church and empire could claim that its power and justice were inscribed in what little was left of Polycarp's charcoaled body.[44] The empire could claim victory because it offers proof of its power in the myth-creating atmosphere of the arena. It could view the remains of Polycarp's body and give glory to itself and its gods for its triumph over the subversive "atheist."

However, the church also claimed victory, because God has promised to separate the sheep from the goats on judgment day (Matt 25:31-34). It is God's promise that those who remain in waiting for God's vindication will wait but "a little longer" (Rev 6:11). It is quite possibly this promise that Saturus envisioned when he told the jeering crowd, "Note our faces diligently, that you may recognize them on that day of judgment."[45] To *live* into one's resurrection is the victory of the martyrs, for it signifies the rejection of the fallen order for the much-hoped-for kingdom of God. Bodily resurrection orders the body *prior* to death and legitimizes the hopes of all Christians who have already started to rise with Christ in their baptism (Rom 6—8).

The Seed Blooms: Resurrection

In bitter argument against those who clung to docetic accounts of Jesus' flesh, Ignatius claimed that if Jesus only appeared to suffer, then neither his death nor Ignatius's martyrdom has any purpose.[46] For Ignatius, Jesus' actual suffering establishes the mimetic model for all those who would follow him to a cross. To entertain notions, therefore, of Jesus merely appearing to suffer while those who imitate him physically do would be to bear false witness, because the martyrs' imitation would be fabricated.[47] Moreover, hopes of a material resurrection, which assumes an inherent good attached to the body that requires liberation from its bondage to sin, would be rendered suspect. As Ignatius put it, "If the Lord were in the body in appearance only, then I am also bound in appearance only."[48] If Jesus did not assume flesh, we must assume that flesh does not require redemption. This, Ignatius claimed, is a falsehood that beckons condemnation.[49]

In his treatise on the resurrection, Justin Martyr addressed those who cast doubt on the possibility of bodily renewal because of their understanding of the flesh as contemptible:

> We must . . . speak with respect to those who think meanly of the flesh, and say that it is not worthy of the resurrection nor of the heavenly economy, because, first, its substance is earth; and besides it is full of all wickedness, so that it forces the soul to sin along with it. But these persons seem to be ignorant of the whole work of God, both of the genesis and formation of man at the first, and why the things in the world were made. For does not the word say, "Let Us make man in our image, and after our likeness?" What kind of man? Manifestly He means fleshly man. For the word says, "And God took dust of the earth, and made man." It is evident, therefore, that man made in the image of God was of flesh. Is it not, then, absurd to say, that the flesh was made by God in His own image is contemptible, and worth nothing? But that the flesh is with God a precious possession is manifest, first from its being formed by Him, if at least the image is valuable to the former and the artist; and besides, its value can be gathered from the creation of the rest of the world. For that on account of which the rest is made, is the most precious of all to the maker.[50]

What is made in the image of God cannot be contemptible to God. The flesh is in the likeness of God and is therefore good.

Justin expected his audience to concur with this much, yet he also heard them ask, "Does not the flesh lead the soul into sin?" He responded by refuting any dualism in which the flesh desecrates the soul. He asks, "But in what instance can the flesh possibly sin by itself, if it have [*sic*] not the soul going before it and inciting it?"[51] Justin does not think it possible that either the soul or the body can act without being in communion with the other. However, if he is wrong, that is, if the flesh is the "sinner," then precisely on its account Christ assumes flesh. God becomes flesh in order that flesh may be saved, and the flesh *is* saved because Jesus' body, Justin reminds us, is no longer in the tomb. The Father raises the Son's body and the Son appears in the flesh to his disciples. "Why did He rise in the flesh in which He suffered," Justin asked, "unless to show the resurrection of the flesh?"[52] Therefore, Christians have no ground on which to argue that the soul, and not the body, is redeemed. For Justin, this meant that Christians must believe in the resurrection of the flesh; otherwise, they assume both that God "labored in vain" with the creation of flesh and that God's creation is not worthy of redemption and restoration.[53]

Irenaeus, in his defense of a material resurrection, connected the dying and rising of the human body with our feeding on the risen Christ:

> When, therefore, the mingled cup and the manufactured bread receives the Word of God, and the Eucharist of the blood and the body of Christ is made, from which things the substance of our flesh is increased and supported, how can they affirm that the flesh is incapable of receiving the gift of God, which is life eternal, which [flesh] is nourished from the body and blood of the Lord, and is a member of Him?—even as the blessed Paul declares in his Epistle to the Ephesians, that "we are members of His body, of His flesh, of His bones." He does not speak these words of some spiritual and invisible man, for a spirit has not bones nor flesh; but [he refers to] that dispensation [by which the Lord became] an actual man, consisting of flesh, and nerves, and bones,—that flesh which is nourished by the cup which is His blood, and receives increase from the bread which is His body.[54]

The Eucharist, for Irenaeus, is what makes the Christian possible. It is also what makes possible the rising of the Christian's body after her death. As the body of each Christian is nourished by the Eucharist in life, so also after death each "shall arise at the appointed time . . . to the glory of God."[55]

Caroline Walker Bynum comments on Irenaeus's fleshy theology of the Eucharist and suggests that for Ireneaus "the proof of our final incorruption lies in our eating God."[56] Precisely because "we are what we eat—that we become Christ by consuming Christ, but Christ can never be consumed—guarantees that our consumption by beasts or fire or by the gaping maw of the grave is *not* destruction."[57] Eating a deity that cannot be consumed resists, for all of these theologians, the kind of spiritualizing of the flesh that denies the material embodiment of Christianity either during or after life. Given that Christians are nurtured on the flesh and blood of Christ, we can and must believe that our own flesh and blood will enjoy everlasting communion with God.

A possible hindrance to this notion of a material resurrection resides in Paul's words that "flesh and blood cannot inherit the kingdom of God" (1 Cor 15:50). Such a comment evokes an image of heaven where the bodies we are accustomed to are absent. The absence of such bodies, however, does not contradict the arguments we have been examining. Rather, such absence acknowledges what it means to have our corruptible bodies transfigured so that we might enjoy the heavenly presence of God.

Paul's enigmatic comments require that we take a look at his favorite metaphor for the resurrection of the body: the seed. Paul states that every "body" is like a seed. For the follower of Christ, though the seed may be sown in dishonor, "it is raised in glory"; though it is "sown in weakness, it is raised in power; it is sown a natural body, it is raised a spiritual body. If there is a natural body, there is also a spiritual body" (1 Cor 15:43-45 NAS). Bynum notes that

> whatever the Pauline oxymoron "spiritual body" means it signifies at least two points: First, the image of the seed invokes a notion of a radical transformation, i.e., the wheat that sprouts from the seed is quite different from the bare seed (1 Cor. 15: 37); and, second, the image asserts some real form of continuity between the seed and the wheat.[58]

Though the wheat is not in the form of the seed, it still comes from the seed. The seed has acquired a new form or body.

Paul also claims, quite resolutely, that if the dead are not raised, our faith is worthless (1 Cor 15:12-18). For him, something "must guarantee that the subject of resurrection is 'us.'"[59] "For if the dead are not raised, then Christ has not been raised" (15:16). Paul argues for the resurrection of all bodies because the preaching of a resurrected messiah necessitates such a claim. Resurrection, for Paul, is the crux of the Christian faith. If Christ is not risen, therein guaranteeing our resurrection, then "those also who have fallen asleep in Christ have perished" (15:18 NAS). Yet "flesh and blood cannot inherit the kingdom." Bynum suggests that Paul argues that heaven "is not merely a continuation of earth. Thus, when Paul says 'the trumpet shall sound . . . and we shall be changed,' he means, with all the force of our everyday assumptions, both 'we' and 'changed.'"[60] Just as Jesus' body both consumes food (Luke 24:43) and walks through doors (John 20:19), we can imagine a genuinely transformed body that, though it maintains continuity with our earthly body, has passed from perishable to imperishable nevertheless.

Tertullian claimed (and not in opposition to Paul) that flesh and blood acquire heaven because in our baptism we begin our new lives in Christ.[61] Tertullian's argument begins with Romans 6, where Paul argues that in baptism we become new creatures in Christ. The "newness" of our baptized selves cannot be understated. We are truly a different creature, and when we rise from the dead we will be incorruptible creatures. Tertullian claimed that Paul was right to state that incorruption will not inherit the kingdom of God, but this does not mean that our bodies will not inherit the kingdom. Flesh and blood are subject to corruption, that is, they are subject to death—and there is no death in God's kingdom. The spiritual bodies found in heaven will not bring with them the corruption of "natural bodies." He stressed, along with Paul, that "in a moment, in the twinkling of an eye," the trumpet will sound and the dead will rise and be forever changed (1 Cor 15:52). The dead, Tertullian reminded his audience, are we. Flesh and blood will rise though it will be changed, as anything corrupt cannot reside within the holy city.[62]

Crucial to understanding the resurrection of the martyr's body is not only that God grants victory over the moment of execution, but also that God grants victory over decay. Resurrection is not simply tied to the martyr's hopes of triumphing over pain and suffering; it is also tied to the triumph over the fragmentation, disintegration, and scattering of the body.[63] Resurrection overcomes more than the fear of death (if this trait can be appropriately attributed to the martyrs); it over-comes the loss of the body.

According to Eusebius, the martyrs in Lyons and Vienne not only endured "punishments beyond all description," but were not even permitted a proper burial. They were subjected to all sorts of "insults" for six days after their deaths, only to have their bodies, ultimately, consumed by fire. Their ashes were then swept into a neighboring river so that "not even a trace of them might be seen on the earth again." Eusebius claimed that this was done in order to "defeat God and rob the dead of their rebirth." He recalled the persecutors' logic for their actions:

> "In order," they said, "that they may have no hope of resurrection—the belief that has led them to bring into this country a new foreign cult and treat torture with contempt, going willfully and cheerfully to their death. Now let's see if they rise again, and if their god can help them and save them from our hands."[64]

A very real concern in the early church existed over whether or not a Christian body that was either cremated or not given a proper burial could still be resurrected. Based on John 5:28-29, Tertullian argued that resurrection is promised to all Christians (and, much to the chagrin of the non-Christians, to them too) regardless of how they die or how their bodies were treated after their deaths.[65] Not only those bodies in tombs that John mentions will be resurrected, for unburied bodies will be raised as well.[66]

Octavius Januarius, in his dispute with the pagan Caecilius, argued in a manner similar to Tertullian's. Answering his critic's skepticism toward the raising of the human body, Octavius asked why one could concede the creation of humans by God but not the re-creation of the same humans by the same God?[67] If we are nothing after death, we merely share this nothingness in common with what we were prior to existence. Since we, like all of creation, are born from nothing, our rising from nothing should not be difficult to imagine.

This has obvious implications for Octavius's understanding of the raising of "dishonored" bodies. Regardless of whether a body is desecrated or not, such desecration in no way affects its restoration. It is simply not necessary for Christians to receive a proper burial (though it is a respectful and good thing to have), because burial does not keep bodies from decaying. In the dialogue, Octavius asked whether

Caecilius believed that if a body were to disappear from his eyes it was also withdrawn from God. "Every body," he continued, "whether it is dried up into dust, or is dissolved into moisture, or is compressed into ashes, or is attenuated into smoke, is withdrawn from us, but it is reserved for God in the custody of the elements."[68] Those who attack the body can do whatever they want with it; it will in no way hinder God from raising it. That the body will be resurrected, despite its scattering and disappearance from the earth, is hardly a task for the One who creates out of nothing.

The Risen One (A Reply to Caecilius)

If Christ has not been raised, our preaching is useless.
                                        —Paul (1 Cor 15:14)

Caecilius asked Octavius:

> I should be glad to be informed whether or no you rise again
> with bodies; and if so, with what bodies—whether with the
> same or with renewed bodies? Without a body? Then, as far as
> I know, there will neither be mind, nor soul, nor life. With the
> same body? But this has already been previously destroyed.
> With another body? Then it is a new man who is born, not the
> former one restored.[69]

Caecilius concludes that there has yet to be an example of one, through
the innumerable ages, who has returned from the dead.

   Christian orthodoxy affirms that there has been one to return from
the dead: Jesus of Nazareth. His return is not as an apparition or a
vision but is bodily. When the eleven recognized that Jesus stood in their
midst, he quickly assured them that they were not "seeing a ghost"
(Luke 24:37). "Look at my hands and my feet; see that it is I myself.
Touch me and see; for a ghost does not have flesh and bones as you see
that I have" (24:39). His physical return invites some of the very difficult questions posed by Caecilius. Jesus returns bodily, yet this body
appears to walk through walls (20:19) as well as disappears (24:31).
Jesus' resurrected body consumes food (24:43) and ascends into heaven
(Mark 16:19). His bodily scars are recognizable to the doubting one
(John 20:27) despite going unrecognized, at first, by others (Luke 24:16;
John 20:15).[70]

   Perhaps the best answer to Caecilius's question is provided by Paul.
Paul addresses the interlocutor's question: "How are the dead raised? And
with what kind of body do they come?" He rather indignantly answers:

> You fool! That which you sow does not come to life unless it
> dies; and that which you sow, you do not sow the body which
> is to be, but a bare grain, perhaps of wheat or of something
> else. But God gives it a body just as He wished, and to each of
> his seeds a body of its own. (1 Cor 15:35-38 NAS)

Paul uses the seed metaphor to depict how our bodies, seemingly annihilated, rise from the dead. The flesh is redeemed (Rom 8:23) but the heavenly body differs from the earthly body: "It is sown a perishable body, it is raised an imperishable body" (1 Cor 15:42 NAS). That the body perishes is "not an obstacle to its continuity, but the necessary condition for its passage into new life."[71]

The martyr's flesh has to be capable of both impassibility and transfiguration if it is going to inherit the kingdom of God. Asceticism and discipleship, predicated on liturgical formation, make the necessary shift from mutability to immutability possible. The final victory, as Bynum puts it, "must be the eating that does not consume, the decay that does not devour, the change that transmutes only to changelessness."[72] Suffering and decay are not the final answer, for we feed on the broken yet risen and glorified body that makes possible our future rising and glorification.

Against those who deny the resurrection, Paul says, "If the dead are not raised, "Let us eat and drink, for tomorrow we die" (1 Cor 15:32). The putting on of a new garment, the change from change to changelessness, or the transformation from corruption to incorruption is promised to us because we eat and drink the resurrected body of Christ. Our bodies will not die tomorrow; rather, they will be completed in God's eternal kingdom.

In this chapter I have attempted to show, via ancient and contemporary Christian writers, why the body, and its resurrection from death, is the site by which political battles are won and lost. Moreover, because the early martyrs were the kind of people whose bodies had to be excluded from and destroyed by the empire, both the martyr's and the executioner's politics are possible. It is this relationship between executioner and martyr, and the kind of political orientation necessary to sustain such a relationship, that I wish to explore further in sixteenth-century Christianity.

Performance:
The Sixteenth-Century Debacle

In 1535 Charles V issued an edict against the group known as the Anabaptists. This was not the first ordinance against the "re-baptizers," but this particular one was a rallying cry. In order to protect "the commandments of our mother the holy church," Charles V required that all officials under his command immediately proclaim his decree

> within every place and border . . . that all those, or such as shall be found polluted by the accursed sect of the Anabaptist . . . shall incur the loss of life and property, and be brought to the most extreme punishment, without delay; namely, those who remain obstinate and continue in their evil belief and purpose . . . shall be punished with fire. All other persons who have rebaptized, or who secretly and with premeditation have harbored any of the aforesaid Anabaptists, and who renounce their evil purpose and belief, and are truly sorry and penitent for it, shall be executed with the sword, and the women shall be buried in a pit.[1]

Such "mercy" from the Christian emperor extended not only to the penitents but also to anyone who interceded on their behalf:

> Moreover, we prohibit all our subjects from asking for mercy, forgiveness, or reconciliation for the aforesaid Anabaptists, or from presenting any petitions for this purpose, on pain of summary punishment; for because of their evil doctrine, we will not have or permit that any Anabaptists shall have any mercy shown

them, but that they shall be punished, as an example unto others, without any dissimulation, favor or delay. And in order to do this with all that pertains to it, we give each and all of you full power and special command.[2]

To even attempt to practice Christian hospitality was an imperial crime.

This was not the first time, however, that Christians had colluded with or made use of imperial power against other Christians. In 304, Roman authorities arrested some Abitinian Christians and placed them in prison to await their execution. As was customary, Christians within the Carthage area visited their imprisoned friends to bring them food and comfort. Their attempt was unsuccessful, however, due to the Christian bishop of Carthage. He ordered that these Christians were to receive no visitors and sent his deacon Caecilian to stop any potential company. Caecilian "struck down" those who attempted to comfort the prisoners.[3] He made sure that the food and drink brought to the prison were scattered about and given to dogs. He kept parents and children alike from the sight of the martyrs-to-be, causing "dreadful weeping" and "bitter lamentation." For this, the narrator of the Abitinian martyrs stated that, in keeping "the pious from the embrace of the martyrs" and by impeding "Christians from a duty of piety, Caecilian was more ruthless than the tyrant, more bloody than the executioner."[4] The narrator identified this fellow Christian as one who had collaborated with power and had turned against his brothers and sisters in Christ.

In 311, Caecilian was ordained bishop. Though seven years had passed, many friends and family members still recalled his actions and protested his election. Also at work in their protest was their claim that some of the members of the hierarchy who made Caecilian's ordination possible were part of the "lapsed." During Diocletian's persecution, many bishops and priests turned over sacred books to be burned and many lay Christians recanted their faith. Following Diocletian's brutal campaign, many of these lapsed came back to the church with little to no (or at least, in the eyes of some, "not enough") penance being served. Those protesting this situation (often pejoratively labeled Purists or Rigorists) ordained a bishop in place of Caecilian: Donatus. This resulted in the split in the African church between those who followed Caecilian and those who followed Donatus.

The dispute between the two groups grew, and Donatism, as a church movement with its own hierarchy and own churches, spread rather successfully. Following "Rome's conversion," Constantine was appealed to in order to settle the matter between the two groups. The Donatists lost the dispute, and because they refused to recognize the imperially backed/funded church, a severe Donatist repression occurred between 317 and 321, as well as from 346 to 348. During these periods, property was taken, bishops were sent into exile and Donatist "martyrs" were created (at one point, an entire congregation was massacred inside a Carthage basilica).[5] This was a crucial event because the conversion of the empire had all but signified the end of the age of martyrs. Yet the age of martyrs, for the Donatists, was still occurring—reinforcing their belief that they were indeed the true church.

The short reign of Julian the Apostate (361-363) instituted a renewed tolerance for Donatism, which eventually led to it being the established church in Numidia. In Hippo, Catholics were in the minority and often paid the price for their minority status. The Donatists were by no means above using its power to quell Catholicism. Financially and legally, it often times behooved Catholics to become Donatists. The Circumcellions, an extreme gypsy-like wing of the Donatists, were quite violent toward Catholics, and in dealing with their own schism in reference to the followers of Maximian, Donatists appealed to imperial laws in order to regain lost churches held by the Maximianist bishops. Some Donatists, it seems, were not above appealing to whatever means necessary in order to protect their own livelihood. Whether it was by appeal to the emperor or actions of violence toward Catholics, particular Donatists often sought to establish their "pure" church on earth.[6]

At the same time, the record is by no means clear that the followers of Donatus should, theologically, have been committed to acts of violent coercion for the sake of their expansion or survival. An individual act of violence was neither a theological strategy nor a reflection upon the thinking of Donatus or certain Donatist bishops.[7] The Donatist memorandum read at the Council of Carthage in 411 opened by stating, "Januarius and the other bishops of the catholic truth that suffers persecution but does not persecute."[8] These opening words suggest innocence in terms of violence and an attempt to position the Catholic Church as the entity that persecuted the truth. The true people of God, claimed the Donatists, have always suffered persecution and always will. One merely had to look at who is persecuting and who is suffering to figure out which side represents the true church.

This was a point of contention between Augustine and his Donatist rivals. In conversation with the Donatist bishop Fortunius, Augustine employed his famous maxim "not the punishment, but the cause makes the martyr," contending that suffering persecution does not necessarily indicate righteousness.[9] Fortunius argued that since they did not persecute, they clearly stood in succession with the prophets, apostles, and early-church Christians—all of whom were persecuted for righteousness' sake. The Donatists attempted to buttress their case by pointing out that it was they who were on the receiving end of a theologically scripted state sword. That Christian emperors were persecuting other Christians merely suggested to them that the emperor and his Catholic Church were standing in continuity with the pagan emperors and their religions prior to Christianity. Donatism persisted, if by nothing else, by the assurance that imperial persecution signified that righteousness and apostolic succession were on their side, while Augustine would continually argue that suffering was not the "most infallible mark of Christian righteousness."[10]

Augustine, the first theologian to give a Christian justification for imperial coercion against non-Catholics, spent an extensive amount of his theological tenure repudiating the Donatists. Admirably hesitant in the beginning, he eventually came to the conclusion that despite the fact that the decision to choose between good and evil was an act of free will, such an act of choice could be prepared for by a lengthy process that employed certain "external" or "medicinal inconveniences" if they increased the chances of conversion.[11] He argued that just as Paul was struck blind by Jesus, so too must heretics not be spared the rod. The fallen servants must be "recalled to their Lord by the stripes of temporal scourging," for just as Paul was healed by his physical punishment, so too could heretics be led to conversion.[12] By arguing for physical coercion, Augustine was not seeking the death of the church's enemies, but rather their salvation from eternal punishment. Though Augustine continually requested that the torture inflicted on Donatists fall short of actual death (in principle, as Peter Brown reminds us, Augustine was opposed to the death penalty), later adaptations of his arguments for corporal punishment would develop into full-blown justifications for the use of capital punishment as a means of dealing with those who refused to be Catholic.[13] If a heretic remained unmoved, her life might be ended so as not to infect others with heresy.

This was, unfortunately, not the only time in church history that Christian blood would be spilled by other Christians; its reappearance in the sixteenth century became almost a matter of course. The reemergence of Christians killing Christians over issues of truth and heresy, issues soteriological in nature, was an all-too-common practice of sixteenth-century Christianity. Departing from the nonviolence of Christianity's early years, the use of violence by Christians against other Christians in the fourth and fifth century, as well as in the sixteenth century, displays a dramatic shift in what it means for how Christians function as political creatures. It is not as important to discover who was doing the most killing between the Catholics and the Donatists in the fourth century, or the Catholics and the Protestants in the sixteenth century, as it is to discover how either group found itself in the position to be persecutor.

Thinking through the monumental shift from being persecuted by a pagan emperor for being a Christian to having Christian emperors persecuting both pagans and other Christians is absolutely crucial for our understanding of martyrdom as an act of political importance. This chapter is not concerned with why and how Christian empires may or may not differ from pagan empires (though the fact that both employ the same methods to eradicate dissent should not be ignored); rather, its concern lies both with understanding what it means for a people to be able to claim legitimate martyrs throughout the age of Christendom and how this shapes our understanding of those people who are either exiled from the city gates or executed within the city gates. That is, are these people martyrs or are they criminals, and what difference does that make in terms of politics?

Though the seeds had already been planted prior to that fateful eve of All Saints of 1517, Luther's pinning of his Ninety-five Theses initiated a rupture in the church that has yet to heal. What began as one monk's attempt among many to call the church to reform resulted in the Reformation, Radical Reformation, Counter-Reformation, and schism after schism. Given the fusion between church and state in the sixteenth century (beginning in the fourth century) all groups, save some of the Radical Reformers, had the apparatus of the state to aid in their quests for agreement on doctrinal issues. If the sixteenth century is known for anything, it is known for the excessive killing that took place *within* the Christian body.[14] Catholics killed Protestants, Protestants killed Catholics, and they both agreed to kill Anabaptists. The victim's ecclesial body cried "martyr" while the inquisitor's ecclesial body cried "criminal." In all three traditions, being a martyr was possible only if one died for true doctrine and, in some cases, semantics were all the difference between being a saint and being a sinner.

What are we to make of the violent measures used by Christians against other Christians (originating with Caecilian and expanding to Augustine's hesitant yet ultimate justification of the persecution of the Donatists)? What are we to make of the fact that "persecution," in this case, occurred not from a pagan sword, but from a Christian sword? What "truths" were Christians dying and killing for and what truth was being promulgated in the actual performance of such dying and killing? Finally, what kind of politics is at work in the desire and achievement of death over doctrine?

Whose Martyrdom, Which Ecclesiology?

For the time is coming when people will not put up with sound doctrine.

—2 Timothy 4:3

Lords: "What do you hold concerning our mass?"
Elizabeth: "My lords, of your mass I think nothing at all; but I highly esteem all that accords with the Word of God."
Lords: "What are your views with regards to the most adorable holy sacrament?"
Elizabeth: "I have never in my life read in the holy Scriptures of a holy sacrament, but of the Lord's Supper." . . .
Lords: "What did the Lord say, when He gave His disciples the Supper?"
Elizabeth: "What did He give them, flesh or bread?"
Lords: "He gave them bread."
Elizabeth: "Did not the Lord remain sitting there? Who then would eat the flesh of the Lord?"
Lords: "What are your views concerning infant baptism, seeing you have been rebaptized?"
Elizabeth: "No, my lords, I have not been rebaptized. I have been baptized once upon my faith; for it is written that baptism belongs to believers."
. . . Sentence was then passed upon Elizabeth, on the 27th of March 1549; she was condemned to death—to be drowned in a bag, and thus offered up her body to God.[15]

This brief interchange between Catholic inquisitors and the captured Anabaptist Elizabeth (mistakenly thought to be the wife of ex-Catholic priest Menno Simons) is famous in Anabaptist martyrology. It gives a good account of what took place in the interrogation processes of the sixteenth century. As the above anecdote suggests, issues such as the mass, baptism, and the Eucharist (and the story of Elizabeth, like so many others, also delve into matters of ecclesial hierarchy, anointing the sick, and confession) were matters worthy of both the infliction and acceptance of death.

To say that Christians were "dying for doctrines" in the sixteenth century is not to say that doctrine had replaced Christ, but since all divergent groups claimed Christ, the only means by which one could discern and test the spirits was through correct teaching of Christ.[16] Each group assumed that it was teaching correctly. It was therefore incapable of recognizing martyrs in other ecclesial camps. If a Protestant were to recognize an executed Catholic as a genuine martyr, she would have to become Catholic—as this would mean that Catholics were practitioners of the true teachings of Christ. The only way for these groups to resolve their conflicts would have been through doctrinal compromise, and ultimately, through a healing of church schisms.

Catholics, Protestants, and Anabaptists all claimed to be dying as witnesses to Christ, and both Catholics and Protestants, in putting each other to death (including the Anabaptists), claimed to be doing the work of God. Precisely because of this, those executed often cited John 16:2: "[A]n hour is coming when those who kill you will think that by doing so they are offering worship to God." All parties agreed that they were dying and killing in faithfulness to God, yet they disagreed in specific matters of doctrine. This meant that the difference between, for example, adhering to transubstantiation and consubstantiation was a matter of life and death.

Though it may seem odd to die or kill over the denial of the literal presence of Christ in the Eucharist, we must not underestimate the immediate link between discipleship and doctrine that rendered such spilling of blood necessary. Sound doctrine is essential, because only correct teaching in reference to God can produce godly actions (1 Tim 4). Clearly, this was no small matter. In the early church, there was no separation between doctrine and ethics (ethics, as a subdiscipline within Christian discourse, had to be invented after this separation).[17] Therefore, to entertain false beliefs automatically posited a life of false activity. The early Christians rightly understood that correct teaching was vital to a life of Christian witness. Such an understanding carried through to the sixteenth century, even if the consequences of maintaining false doctrines (or at least ones in disagreement with those in power) produced results that were antithetical to the heart of Christianity (that is, the love and forgiveness of one's enemies).[18]

Issues of doctrinal truth versus heterodox postures have been a central concern in the church since the first century. The New Testament stresses adherence to correct teaching (doctrine), and the Ante-Nicene writers were often quite pointed in their remonstrations against those who deviated from very specific teachings. The danger of heresy is not that it just destroys the heretic, but that it is like a plague: once it has spread it is capable of destroying thousands of lives. Heresy, therefore, is the most dangerous kind of sin, for it not only destroys the heretic but also functions like a contagious disease—infecting others through contact. It was for this reason that the sixteenth-century church felt so strongly the need to stamp it out.[19] Eternal separation from God was not something easily dismissed in the late medieval ages. Hell was not simply an existential or symbolic state of being. Rather, it was that place where those who die outside of communion with the church spend eternity. It was therefore for the protection of her body that the church could not simply allow false teachings to go unpunished. By the time of the Reformation (indeed, well before), heresy had become a crime punishable by death.

That heresy was both a sin and a crime for the sixteenth-century Christian is significant. In *Salvation at Stake: Christian Martyrdom in Early Modern Europe*, Brad Gregory makes a crucial distinction between *persecuted* Christians and *prosecuted* Christians.[20] Both Catholic and Protestant authorities were not bent upon persecuting "innocent" Christians but on prosecuting religious criminals. Indeed, for the orthodox there was nothing innocent about a religious deviant. The heterodox, inasmuch as they maintained a posture outside of doctrinal orthodoxy, were bearing, in both word and deed, false witness to God. Heresy was not simply a matter of inward corruption, because Christians lived what they believed.

Hans Hergot was executed in 1527 on the charge of sedition for distributing a pamphlet called *The New Transformation of Christian Living*. The title of the tract itself suggests that Christians were not killed simply because of ideas. Rather, Christians were constructing new ways of living based on their divergent understandings of the sacraments, ecclesial hierarchy, and subjection to temporal authority. If, as the Anabaptists argued, infant baptism was a corruption of discipleship, then their convictions automatically implied a different practice in terms of this sacrament. Such beliefs led to counter-cultural practices that undermined, intentionally or not, the very fabric of Christendom. They posed a serious threat to the social order because they required one to break from her ecclesial bonds. This break disrupted the social structure, for it questioned the very legitimacy of that from which so-called secular authority derived its power.

By leaving the Catholic Church, for example, both Protestants and

Anabaptists were not only stating that Catholicism was errant (and this is putting it mildly) but also that the temporal powers that were supposed to be under the judgment of the church were also misled. This did not make the Protestants anarchists, for though the reformers questioned much, they did not question the basic church-state bonds of the medieval period. The Anabaptists, on the other hand, never denied their subjection to temporal power; they simply argued that the enforcing of temporal power required a kind of commitment that was at odds with the way of Christ.

Eventually, Catholics separated themselves to Catholic regions and Protestants separated themselves to Protestant regions, with the nomadic Anabaptists roaming between the two. Catholics captured in Protestant regions as well as Protestants found in Catholic regions were guilty of heresy and/or sedition. Edmund Campion was paraded through Protestant London with a paper fixed upon his hat that stated in large capital letters: "Campion, The Seditious Jesuit." Immediately prior to his execution he prayed for the conversion of his executors as well as the Protestant church that made his martyrdom possible.[21] On the other side, Catholic authorities sentenced two English Protestants to be burned to death for treason. The crippled Hugh Laverock assured the blind John Apprice that the "good physician of London" would cure them after their deaths. Jesus, according to these martyrs, was a Protestant from London.[22]

With no "ruler to call their own,"' Anabaptists lacked the power to protect themselves against Catholic or Protestant law. Despite being a peaceful group, or perhaps because they forsook the weapons and oaths necessary to carry them, they were charged with sedition, subversion, and the destruction of the social order by both Catholics and Protestants. By insisting upon the notion of the church as a voluntary community separate from the civil community, Anabaptists undermined eleven hundred years of established Christian practice. Neither Catholics nor Protestants tolerated such destructive behavior, and the death penalty was practiced against those who underwent a second baptism.

This second baptism, heresy according to both the Catholics and Protestants, resulted in the death of Anabaptists more because of its subversive nature than its heretical content (though concepts like heresy and subversion cannot be neatly separated in the sixteenth century). For instance, though Martin Luther argued against the death penalty in cases of heresy ("he will have his punishment enough in hell fire"), he did contend that capital punishment was necessary in cases of sedition:

"Although it seems cruel to punish them with the sword, it is crueler that they condemn the ministry of the Word and have no well-grounded doctrine and suppress the true and in this way seek to subvert the civil order."[23] Heresy led to sedition, and this disrupted the social order given for the protection of the weak and the punishment of the wicked. What frightened Luther and others most about the Anabaptists was their denial of the possibility of a territorial church.

The influential Schleitheim Articles, penned by ex-Benedictine priest Michael Sattler, were appalling in the eyes of many Protestants and Catholics as they imagined the articles would create chaos.[24] Sattler's seven articles discussed baptism, the ban, the breaking of bread, separation from abomination, shepherds in the congregation, the sword, and the oath.[25] Most troublesome to non-Anabaptists was the notion of how believers baptism led one to treat earthly allegiances as merely relative: Christians are subordinate to the government yet are not expected to practice obedience to any government that asks of its citizens something that is incongruent with the gospel. This is, by no means, a novel claim. That the Christian's first loyalty is to Christ is a claim that most other Christians would hardly deny. What made Sattler's understanding of loyalty to Christ problematic in terms of civil authority was that implied following Christ in *all* things. This meant that just as Christ did not employ the sword, neither should his followers.

The pacifism of Sattler's articles undermined the social order because it was predicated on the assumption that Christians could not serve as magistrates or executioners. Such activity, argued Sattler, is outside the perfection of Christ. Not only should Christians not practice these vocations, but they also must separate themselves from any activity connected to secular authority (for example, by not taking others to court). By refusing to take the oath, by not holding governmental office, and by not carrying the sword, Anabaptists, despite being peaceful, were charged with sedition of the order that God had created and were therefore not only seditious but also guilty of blasphemy (heresy and treason often went hand in hand).

Though Sattler never denied that temporal power was subject to God's authority, he did deny that it was congruent with Christian discipleship, which got him burned at the stake. The danger of Sattler and of Anabaptists in general was not just their lack of emphasis on the objective nature of the sacraments, but their ability to create alternative communities premised on a radical understanding of the gospel.

Their understanding of the holding of goods in common, their general mistrust of private property, and their refusal to defend themselves or the social order were akin to monastics attempting to make their life the norm for all Christians.[26] Such a blurring of distinctions within Christianity as well as the distinction between the planes of temporal and earthly authority threatened the good of all and received an immediate response of criminal prosecution.

So, the distinction between prosecution and persecution is important in order to understand the inquisitor's worldview. It is also important, however, to note that those on the receiving end of prosecution understood it to be persecution. Though Catholics and Protestants justified their violent treatment of each other as forms of criminal prosecution, all those suffering prosecution understood it to be in accord with the biblical witness that relabeled it persecution.

For example, deeply disturbed by the large number of his people being "prosecuted" and hence subjected to the death penalty, John Calvin responded against the "disgrace of shedding so much innocent blood" and labeled their deaths "murder." These deaths Calvin called "precious in the sight of the Lord," because these Christians were saints who, like the Lamb they followed, were persecuted for righteousness' sake, not legitimately prosecuted for being criminals.[27] Such examples as this are countless on all three sides. No Christians were willing to be charged with persecution, for what kind of Christian persecutes the church? Likewise, no persecuted Christian wished to be understood as being prosecuted, for that would legitimate the claims made by the prosecutors.

Nevertheless, because such a distinction did exist, it produced, or rather perpetuated, a sense of what constituted political and apolitical activities. For example, in our present era, many are inclined to favor the Anabaptists because they embodied a more "tolerant" position: they were persecuted, yet persecuted no one. Four to five centuries ago, however, they were heavily criticized *for this very reason*. The Anabaptists were charged with a lack of charity because they "neglected their duty" by refusing to participate in the prosecution of those who differed from their doctrines.[28] This was both theologically and politically a scandal. Theologically, if the Anabaptists were so convinced that they embodied right doctrine, why did they not attempt to coerce false believers away from certain damnation? Such neglect or absence of charity suggests that they lacked genuine love for their enemies and therefore could not have been of the true church. Politically, this was scandalous because the Anabaptists forsook the good of the temporal order by appearing to advocate withdrawal into enclaves of would-be perfectionists.[29]

The issue of what comprises the difference between persecution and prosecution, and how we understand the kind of politics such a distinction demands, brings us full circle. To determine which side prosecuted and which persecuted requires a verdict on whose doctrines were authentic. Yet how could such a verdict be rendered, especially without an entire ecclesial tradition (or two) admitting to killing disciples of Christ? To persecute the friends of Christ is to persecute Christ; what kind of church persecutes itself? Moreover, is it possible to locate genuine martyrdoms without chalking up entire ecclesial traditions, as all three groups did, to being servants of the antichrist?

Of course, part of being the church is the ability to recognize sin and repent of it. Yet who does the repenting, and does such repentance demand the kind of penance that could result in a major shift in ecclesiology as well as the kind of doctrines that should have prohibited the killing of one another in the first place? If twenty-first-century ecclesial bodies have any chance of reconciliation, the ability to name the martyrs that resulted from these schisms is of utmost importance. The question remains: how do we name these witnesses and how does such naming affect previous and current church doctrines?

Who Do You Say I Am?
(On Locating Visible Performances of the Church)

So are you saying that human agreement decides what is true and what is false?—It is what human beings say that is true and false; and they agree in the language *they use. That is not agreement in opinions but in form of life.*

—Ludwig Wittgenstein

In the historical conflict in which the martyr finds himself, his deed is word, and his word, deed.

—H. von Campenhausen

In *The Nature of Doctrine*, George Lindbeck essayed to provide the resources necessary to "envision the possibility of doctrinal reconciliation without capitulation."[30] As an exercise or experiment in ecumenical theology, Lindbeck endeavored to provide the groundwork for reconciling opposing doctrines without changing their substance. So, for instance, it might be possible for traditions that hold doctrines of transubstantiation and nontransubstantiation to be reconciled without suffering loss of their objective content. If, as I have argued, a major impetus behind martyrdom in the sixteenth century was irreconcilable doctrines, then viewing those rival traditions in light of Lindbeck's work could reshape ongoing discussions of martyrdom within the sixteenth century. That is, it might be possible to resolve particular doctrinal disagreements that led to the killing of Christians by other Christians without simultaneously undoing the very substance of the doctrines that many of these Christians found worthy of their lives.

Lindbeck proposed three prominent types of the theological relationship between belief and doctrine: cognitive-propositionalism, experiential-expressivism, and an unnamed combination of the two.[31] The cognitive-propositionalist maintains that if a doctrine is once true then it is always true. Church doctrines function as informative propositions about objective realities. In the case of the Eucharist, either the bread is Christ's flesh or it is not. There is no "both/and" solution, and to admit one way or the other is to establish the parameters of an ecumenical conversation before it even begins.[32] Such a position does not hold much hope for the possibility of doctrinal reconciliation without serious compromise. In the case of rival martyrs, this would imply the possibility of certain martyrs having their status as martyrs removed.[33]

By way of contrast, the experiential-expressivist maintains that the significance of a doctrine depends more on the meaning attributed by the individual subject to that doctrine. The doctrine, while remaining unchanged, can produce a variety of meanings in each different person without the doctrine itself being altered. Lindbeck continued to use the example of transubstantiation and claimed that under this model one's belief in the literal transformation of elements in the Eucharist is not as important as the "conceptualities" that "evoke similar or dissimilar experiences of divine reality, or no experience at all."[34] Doctrine, under this model, is not critical for agreement or disagreement because it expresses the fundamental experiences or attitudes of agents and not an ontological truth associated with a certain ecclesial body's teaching. In this sense, there is no final objective meaning, and it is not clear why there should be any meaning at all except for what the individual or community accords to it.

The third model, a synthesis of the two, incorporates both propositionalist and experiential-expressivist perspectives and is better equipped for ecumenical purposes than the first two types. Lindbeck, however, argued that this position has difficulty coherently combining the two. He claimed that because such a theory, represented primarily by ecumenically minded Roman Catholics, is "weak in criteria for determining when a given doctrinal development is consistent with the sources of faith," theorists of this sort must rely on the official teaching of the magisterium in a way that their interlocutors are probably not willing to concede.[35]

Finding these three unhelpful, Lindbeck provided an alternative, based largely on the philosophical work of Ludwig Wittengestein, which he called the cultural-linguistic model. In this system, religion resembles a language with its concomitant doctrines functioning as rules, the grammar of the language. Doctrines are to be understood not as expressive symbols (because doctrine makes "subjective" experience possible) or as truth claims per se; rather, doctrines function as "communally authoritative rules of discourse, attitude, and action" that find their intelligibility in their use.[36] Language, for the cultural linguist, does not represent life; rather, to visualize language is to already visualize a "form of life" that makes language work. If religion can be likened to a language, Lindbeck argued, it can be understood as a communal phenomenon that shapes the subjectivities of individuals rather than being primarily a manifestation of those subjectivities. It comprises a vocabulary of discursive and nondiscursive symbols together with a distinctive logic or grammar in terms of which this vocabulary can be meaningfully deployed.[37]

For example, one can see that the command "Drive on the right side of the road" could mean various things. It may mean that one should drive on the right, as opposed to left, side of the road, or it could mean that one should drive on the correct side of the road (if one were driving in England, for instance, "right" would be the left side). To speak is to inhabit a form of life that makes such speech possible. This form of life is at least partly constituted by a certain grammar that renders language comprehensible to both the speaker and the audience. In similar fashion, doctrine functions as the basic grammar that makes being a Christian possible. Without grammar, without "rules of speech" within Christianity, being a Christian would be meaningless, for we would not know what being a Christian means.

For Lindbeck, employing the cultural-linguistic model makes doctrinal reconciliation possible without capitulation by specifying when, where, and how such rules apply. Returning to his example of the Eucharist, he suggested that conflicting doctrines on what happens with the elements

> can be interpreted as embodying rules of sacramental thought and practice that may have been unavoidable and perhaps irresolvable collision in certain historical contexts, but that can be harmonized by appropriate specifications of their respective domains, uses and priorities. In short, to the degree that doctrines function as rules . . . there is no logical problem in understanding how historically opposed positions can in some, even if not all, cases be reconciled while remaining in themselves unchanged.[38]

Lindbeck believed that doctrinal reconciliation without capitulation is possible through this model. He proposed a theory by which ecumenically minded Christians can begin to reconcile without compromising the memories of those who died for what seem to be irreconcilable differences.

Whether Lindbeck's cultural linguisticism "works" has been hotly contested since its publication.[39] It is not my task to argue for its promise in the field of ecumenics, nor am I wholly convinced that a little capitulation is a bad idea. Rather, what I find most helpful about his work is his account of how a statement can be both true and false. To furnish his reader with such an account, Lindbeck dinstinguished between the intrasystematic and the ontological truth of statements. Intrasystematic truth is a function of coherence, while ontological truth pertains to the correspondence to reality that is attributable to first-order propositions.

Lindbeck claimed that our utterances are "intrasystematically true when they cohere with the total relevant context, which, in the case of religion when viewed in cultural-linguistic terms, is not only utterances but also the correlative forms of life."[40] Therefore, the Christian claim that God is Three in One is "true only as [a part] of a total pattern of speaking, thinking, feeling, and acting." Such a statement is false when its "use in any given instance is inconsistent with what the pattern as a whole affirms of God's being and will."[41] Lindbeck continued:

> The crusader's battle cry "*Christus est Dominus*," for example, is false when used to authorize cleaving the skull of the infidel (even though the same words in other contexts may be a true utterance). When employed, it contradicts the Christian understanding of Lordship as embodying, for example, suffering servanthood.[42]

In other words, for Christian claims to make sense they cannot be detached from behavior. Thus, the crusader's claim of Christ's lordship is intrasytematically false. To claim Christ as Lord while simultaneously "cleaving the skull of the infidel" is to speak untruthfully. Such speech, accompanied by a contradictory action, is intrasystematically incoherent.

In Lindbeck's view, language is performative. To claim one thing yet engage in an activity that contradicts it is to render the claim false. This has important repercussions for how we attempt to make sense of the statement made by all three traditions that "Christ is Lord." Is this a truthful statement when sung from the lips of the person burning at the stake? Or is it a truthful statement when pronounced by the clergy responsible for the person burning at the stake? Perhaps both could be true or both could be false.[43] The difficulty lies in understanding how such an utterance may or may not be intelligible in light of the kind of world one inhabits. For the former, it makes sense to sing "Christ is Lord" while being executed, for it bespeaks continuity with the way of the slaughtered Lamb. The latter, however, can also claim "Christ is Lord," because the death of the church's enemies represents Christ's ultimate victory over evil. The task lies in one's understanding of who Jesus is and how that understanding is answered performatively.

To answer verbally that Jesus is Lord would not have been a terribly difficult task during sixteenth-century Christendom. Even during our post-Christendom era, to answer that Jesus is Lord is hardly difficult. Whether or not this is answered *truthfully*, however, requires that our practices cohere with such a claim. According to Lindbeck, if the claim "Christ is Lord" is to be both intrasystematically and ontologically true, the form of life and understanding of the world "shaped by an authentic use of the Christian stories" must correspond with God's being and will.[44] To state it plainly, if we make the claim that we know Jesus, or that Jesus is our friend, yet for whatever reason do not obey his teachings, then according to Jesus we are liars. "In such a person," states Jesus, "the truth does not exist" (1 John 2:4). If our practices are not consistent with the claims we make, our speech is unintelligible.

Perhaps this is the key to discerning true and false claims between sixteenth-century Christians. Those who are friends of Christ, according to the standard of friendship that Christ himself demands, are those in whom truth exists. Yet how do we know if we are friends of Christ? According to Scripture, friendship is dependent upon obedience: "Now by this we can be sure that we know him, if we obey his commandments" (1 John 2:3). Friendship with Jesus requires obedience. We know truth by knowing Jesus, and we know Jesus by following Jesus. Truth is knowable only through the performance of the way of Christ. Though there remains the task of what constitutes appropriate performance or obedience to Christ, if we can at least agree that disobedience to Christ renders our claims of friendship with him false, we can begin to sort through this quagmire.

This solution, admittedly, merely restates the question: Were the Catholics and Protestants obedient to Christ when they killed subversive heretics, or were the Anabaptists rendering truthful statements about their friendship with Jesus when they were killed yet killed no one?[45] Lindbeck reminds us that there are "no circumstances in which Christians are commanded not to love God or neighbor."[46] All three traditions are, to the best of their understanding, attempting to embody such a command. According to the Catholic and Protestant traditions, the killing of subversives was an act of charity; it was an act of obedience that embodied the command to love both God and neighbor. For the Anabaptists, to kill anyone would be to cease knowing Jesus, because knowledge of Jesus demands obedience to Jesus (1 John 2:4-5), especially in the arduous task of loving one's enemies. The difficulty lies in discerning which ecclesial tradition knows and hence bears witness to Jesus.

Apostolic Succession (A Rather Bloody One)

The question now will be, in what church the true apostolic doctrine has been held from the beginning and is still held; which is a privilege boasted by many.

—Thieleman J. van Braght

Whoever says, "I abide in him," ought to walk just as he walked.

—1 John 2:6

The purpose of the Anabaptist encyclopedia of martyrs, *Martyrs Mirror*, is twofold: first, to provide a treatment of baptism and, second, to give an account of those who died giving witness to Christ, starting with the martyrdom of Stephen and ending in 1660. In this way, late-seventeenth-century Anabaptists attempted to suggest a historical continuity with those who came before them. *Martyrs Mirror* records what many Anabaptists considered to be authentic martyrdoms from the first century until the seventeenth. It intended to mark visibly the "true church of God, its origin, progress, and immovable stability, through all times."[47] In this sense, a historical succession of Christianity can be mapped, linking the Anabaptists back to the early church.

The editor of *Martyrs Mirror*, Thieleman J. van Braght, argued that true succession is found in people who embody true doctrine. This again is the dilemma sixteenth-century Christians faced. All claimed succession because all claimed authentic doctrine. Van Braght stated, "The question will now be, in what church the true apostolic doctrine has been held from the beginning, and is still held; which is a privilege boasted of by many."[48] To describe the content of the Anabaptist faith, van Braght confessed the Apostles' Creed. While doing this underscored the major commonality of Anabaptist movements with both Catholicism and Protestantism, it also suggests that the relevant arguments concerning doctrine were not so much over content as interpretation. This is where the matter of performance becomes important, for if all three traditions confessed the Apostles' Creed—if, in effect, all three said, "*Christus est Dominus*"—then how could it be that they all called each other heretics and even antichrists as they killed or were killed by each other?

Van Braght answered that there are two different bodies of people, each with their own succession, that constitute the world: the people of God (and of heaven) and the people of Satan (and of earth).[49] One group lives in faithfulness to God while the other rejects the way of God. This stark contrast is marked by a different succession within the two bodies. The church, which "is the separated holy flock and people of God," originated with the beginning of the world, has existed through all times, and will continue to exist until the end of the world.[50] What began with Adam led to Noah, from Noah to Abraham, from Abraham to Moses, from Moses to David, from David to Christ, and from Christ to the church. The church, as the body of Christ, is Christ to the world because Christ is in the church. The church, because it reveals Christ, must be visible, for in order to bear witness to the world it must be discernible from the world. This is to say that the church, if it is to be the church, must be distinguishable from all that is not the church. This, according to van Braght, has always been and always will be the case.[51] For the sixteenth-century Anabaptist it did not matter whether you lived in a pagan society like second-century Rome or in the Christendom of the medieval ages, for the church must always be distinguishable from that which is not the church.

The account by Menno Simons, who is quoted often in *Martyrs Mirror*, of this "two peoples" narrative carries an even more intense invective. He stated that, since the beginning of the world, "genuine righteousness and devout piety have been in this way miserably hated, persecuted, cast out and killed, as has been abundantly shown in the case of the early pious fathers and may be seen and found also in these last times." It is absolutely necessary, Simons contended, that those who persecute Christians be revealed for who they really are:

> These are not Christians but an unbelieving, carnal, earthly, wanton, blind, hardened, lying, idolatrous, perverted, malicious, cruel, unmerciful, frightful, and murderous people, who by their actions and fruits show that they neither know Christ nor His Father, even though they so highly praise His holy name with their mouth and extol it with their lips. This is a people that walk in slippery, crooked, and perverted paths, that know nothing of Christian love and peace, that bathe their hearts and hands in blood and are born to seize and kill. They are children and accomplices of him who from the beginning was a murderer and a liar.[52]

For the Anabaptist, and the sixteenth-century Christian in general, one either stemmed from and belonged to God or descended from and belonged to Satan. One could not belong to both. In terms of knowing who belonged where, for the Anabaptist it was evident by the fact that they were the ones suffering persecution, which, like Jesus, they willingly accepted.

This does not mean that there have not been, and will not continue to be, difficulties in distinguishing between the two peoples. One of the continuities that marks the history of God's people is the fact that its visibility is often obscured. The church of God, claimed van Braght, "though never perishing entirely, does not always show herself in her full form, yea, at times, she seems to have vanished altogether, yet not in all, but only in some places."[53] This obscured witness is either due to sloth on the part of the believers or to doctrinal errors that lead the faithful astray. In this sense the church is like an eclipsed moon or the sun behind the clouds: it is occasionally concealed from sight. This notion of partial concealment is carefully qualified by van Braght:

> We do not mean the church in general, or in all places, for the church in general has never been obscured and hidden in all places at the same time; but we mean thereby some parts of the church in general, namely, some particular societies, belonging to the body of the general church which is spread over the whole earth.[54]

He continued by adding that the church of which he spoke was not all those churches that bear the name Christian but only those "who express the Christian name by their upright faith and pure observance of the Christian and Evangelical commandments."[55] The task of *Martyrs Mirror* is thus to trace the continuity with God's people through time. Through two forms of succession, personal and doctrinal, the Anabaptists insisted they were descendants of Abel, Daniel, Peter, and the rest of that "great cloud of witnesses" by presenting, as an argument, biographical examples.[56]

Van Braght traced the historical continuity of the Anabaptists back to the early church by including all those who held a "proper" understanding of baptism. By this he meant that only those who were baptized upon faith could be considered Christian martyrs. As a performance, baptism makes possible the later performance of one's second baptism: the baptism of blood. Such "baptism-minded" people were to be found in every century prior to the sixteenth, and it is with these groups (such as the Lollards and Waldensians) that the Anabaptists found continuity.[57]

Moreover, because their baptism signified belief, repentance, and a conscious decision to follow Christ, the baptism-minded will be persecuted by the world. "If they persecuted me, they will persecute you," claimed Jesus (John 15:20). For the Anabaptists, their baptism of water—an act of civil disobedience that immediately implied execution—was primarily intelligible because it assumed the possibility of the baptism of blood. Their baptisms affirmed their decisions to follow Jesus in order to know Jesus, and such following implied the cross. For the Anabaptists, to go to the cross meant the rejection of any means to save oneself from the cross, but it especially meant rejecting the sword. Just as Jesus did not take up the sword, neither should his followers.

The only sword Christians may wield is that which proceeds from the mouth of the Lord: "If Christ fights his enemies with the sword of His mouth . . . and if we are to be conformed unto His image, how can we, then, oppose our enemies with any other sword?"[58] As the early Christians imagined themselves doing battle against Rome, all without weapons, so too did the Anabaptists of the sixteenth century do battle against other Christians. This is in continuity with the way of God's people. Just as God's prophets Isaiah, Jeremiah, Zechariah, and Amos rebuked with proper teaching and not weapons, so too do Christians rebuke the world. "This same sword," claimed Simons, "we bear and we will lay it down for no emperor or king, magistrate or mayor; for Peter says we ought to obey God rather than men." He continued:

> That this world seeks to change this faithful service of pure love into sedition, this we will have to accept and bear with patience as did our forefathers. . . . Jeremiah, on account of his faithful warning and salutary admonition, had to pass for a rebel and a heretic. Christ Jesus had to hang on a cross. Paul and the apostles had to be clapped into prison as deceivers and conspirators, and in the end had to suffer martyrdom. If now the world could pass a true sentence, then it would acknowledge how that not Christ and His followers were seditious toward the world, *but that the world was seditious toward Christ and His followers.* It would acknowledge that we do not rise against anyone in mutiny, but that the whole world rises up against us in mutiny, tyranny, and "holy war," as may be seen.[59]

The rebel/heretic Jeremiah, the imprisoned Paul, and the crucified Jesus are the ones not to be declared seditious, Simons proclaimed; rather, those who pass judgment against them and their descendants also pass judgment against themselves. The world rises against those who wield the spiritual sword, for it is the kind of sword that delivers the deepest blow: the truth. In the sixteenth century, many swords drew blood, and by the drawing of blood we find Jesus only in those whose blood was drawn. Jesus' blood is a blood that never spills blood—it is a blood that can only be spilt. For the Anabaptists, Christ was being crucified again through his people. This time, it went under the guise of legal prosecution, a justification reminiscent of Pilate washing his hands while the crowds continued to mock.

Those that "prosecuted" the Anabaptists justified their actions by claiming it was lawful. Sedition could not go unpunished, for it destabilized the temporal order. In reply, Simons, who was aware that the rulers imagined themselves to be Christians, asked if a comparison might be drawn between the ways of the emperor and the ways of Christ. Does the emperor walk as Christ walked? Does he obey Christ and do as he specifically taught?[60] If not, Christians should be under no obligation to obey a ruler who rules contrary to the way of Christ. Unfortunately, argued Simons, the emperor is held in higher honor than Christ, yet those who hold the emperor in such esteem still wish to be Christians: "Oh, that the emperor and his aides were Christians, as we so earnestly wish! Then much innocent blood would be spared; blood which is now spilt like water, contrary to all Scripture, reasonableness, and love." Simons asked, "Where have you read a single letter in the whole activity of Christ that men should punish to the blood for the sake of faith, and execute with the sword? Where have the apostles ever taught or practiced such?"[61] Because there is no evidence that Christ, his apostles, or his early followers thought it appropriate to kill their enemies, neither should Christians in the sixteenth century.

This is a key tenet of Simon's teaching that links the Anabaptists with the early church. The Anabaptists did not take up arms against their enemies, because Christ and the early Christians lived lives of nonviolence. This group of Christians, who believed in the Apostles' Creed like all the others, performed this creed by living the way of Christ.[62] They may have entertained, arguably, some "different" ideas in reference to Christology, the Eucharist, or ecclesiology (proof, I think, that Anabaptists require the presence of Protestants and

Catholics as much as Protestants and Catholics require the witness of the Anabaptists), they lived lives that revealed Jesus.

This is not to say that "turning the other cheek" is the only way to show Jesus, but it was a hallmark of early Christianity. Perhaps what is so revolutionary about Christianity is the manner in which it demands that we treat our enemies—and how we treat them reveals whether or not we "show" Jesus. Killing heretics (as enemies of the church *par excellence*) may or may not be good strategy, and it may or may not reveal concern for the common good. These questions can be debated to no end. What is important, however, is whether or not the killing of those deemed heretical shows Jesus in the performance of the killing itself. That is, does being on the giving end of execution show Jesus? The Anabaptists denied that it could and even suggested that only Satan's minions could authorize the killing of God's people (and even if it could be proven that the Anabaptists were not "God's people," this still, in their eyes, would not legitimate the taking of their enemies' lives by Catholic and Protestant authorities).

The Anabaptists gained much credibility precisely on this point of treatment of one's enemies. They dared not persecute or prosecute, for either action would deter one from the path of Jesus. They also did not find themselves in positions in which persecution or prosecution could even be temptations. Not only did this breed of Christian eschew such temptations, but they also only provoked their deaths because of their faith. For those listed in *Martyrs Mirror*, this meant dying as a witness to Christ without any violent provocation on the act of the martyr. What landed one at the stake was simple obedience to the nonviolent way of Jesus.

The continuity Anabaptism attempts to name within salvation history is based on those Christians who, upon baptism of faith, lived lives of faithful obedience to God, implying for them following in footsteps of Jesus. Politically, this necessitated the notion of being a pilgrim people. Like the early nomadic disciples, Christians do not find a permanent home in any earthly polis, but roam through and endure this time and space, providing a glimpse of that eternal city that all of creation is destined to inhabit.[63] This city cannot be found on earth, even though it is often parodied.[64] Christians are called to witness to this heavenly city while seeking the peace of the earthly city (Jer 29:7) yet not calling it home. For the Anabaptists, this implied the theological inability of the church to find a home in a particular province or region because such a territorial understanding limits what the church is and what it can be for the world. The church transgresses all national boundaries, and these nomadic Christians refused to accept the sectarianism of the territorial church.

Martyrs Mirror itself testifies to the way God's people endure both time and space by recording the history of God's actions through God's people of different times, lands, and nationalities. This anthology of martyrs was intended to be not only an inspiration and an exhortation to those facing persecution, but also a gift for those generations that came after it. It is a biographical narrative that aids the contemporary Christian in understanding exactly what apostolic succession is, so that those in the now can better realize what it means to be a Christian in any culture. Regardless of one's traditional or national affiliation, through every century God will reveal who God is through God's people.

The golden age of martyrdom (the first three centuries) happened because of a world hostile to the nonviolent embodiment of the gospel. It was not just "rigorists" like Tertullian who suggested that persecution was a necessity; rather, Jesus himself claimed that if we are to follow him, we must expect no better treatment than the one he received. Paul agreed: "Indeed, all who want to live a godly life in Christ Jesus will be persecuted" (2 Tim 3:12).[65] Persecution, according to Jesus and Paul, hardly seemed optional, so much so that the fourteenth-century Roman Catholic Geert Grote claimed:

> What more? Does not the right and necessary way to the kingdom lead through distress? Does not Scripture say "Many are the tribulations of the righteous" (Ps 33/34: 20/19) and we must "go through many trials to enter the kingdom of God" (Acts 14:22)? And again: "All who want to live piously in Christ Jesus will suffer persecution" (2 Tim 3:12). "So if they persecuted Christ, will they not also persecute you" (John 15:20)? "The disciple is not superior to his master" (Matt 10:24). "Was it not necessary for Christ to suffer and thus to enter into his glory" (Luke 24:26)? Is it not necessary for us Christians, for whom Christ suffered, "also to suffer and continuously bear about in these our mortal bodies the mortification of Christ, so that the life of Jesus be made manifest in our bodies"? . . . For this reason, the Prince of Apostles says, "Christ suffered for us leaving us an example, that we might follow in his steps" (1 Pet 2:21),

so that we might be made "heirs of God and coheirs of Christ, for if we suffer with Him," the Apostle told the Romans, "we will be glorified with him" (Rom 8:17).[66]

Those who follow Christ, go in his footsteps. Though the path that Christians take is not an easy one, they nevertheless embark on a trail that has already been blazed. They go the way of Jesus because it is the only way to go. Just prior to being drowned, Anna Jansz wrote a note to her son, indicating that just as she had decided to take the path of Christ, so should he: "Look, I go the way of the prophets, apostles, and martyrs to drink the cup they all drank, Matt 20:23. I go the way, I say, that Christ Jesus . . . who himself is life and went this way, and not another."[67]

In the earlier case of the Donatists, perhaps their greatest act of betrayal of the gospel was neither their treatment of the lapsed nor their radical understanding of being separate from the world, but their disobedience to Jesus in the form of retaliation that rid them of a visible witness to the peaceableness of God's kingdom.[68] Visible performances of Christianity have a way of narrating our claims better than our best words. In the case of the sixteenth-century Christians, this does not necessarily solve the debate (and perhaps solving the debate is not only not necessary but also not even, ultimately, desirable)[69] but it does give us something by which we can discern which acts are good, beautiful, and true. Maybe then it is possible to distinguish the difference between a pseudo-politics located in earthly regimes and an authentic politics constituted by nothing other than the broken yet risen body of Christ.

Performing Jesus

Bound to a cart pulled by horses, Leonard Keyser, a Lutheran, leaned over and plucked a flower from the field. He showed the flower to his executioners and proclaimed that if they could burn both him and the flower, he would admit to being justly condemned. However, if his body, along with the flower, is not consumed, they should think about what they "have done and repent."

Immediately a fire was built and Keyser, along with his flower in hand, was thrown into it. Neither Keyser nor the flower was burned. A second, larger fire was made, only to produce the same results: Keyser and his flower could not be consumed. Finally, one of the executioners cut his body into pieces, threw them into a new fire (in which they still did not burn), and then cast them in a river.

The story of Leonard Keyser is interesting. Regardless of the authenticity of the "facts" concerning the fireproof Keyser and flower, that he lived and was executed for heresy is unquestioned. What makes this tale interesting is the one telling it: an Anabaptist narrator. This story is found in *Martyrs Mirror*.[70]

Although I have argued in favor of the sixteenth-century Anabaptists, it is important to note how the story of Keyser teaches us a valuable lesson. In this case, the Anabaptists do not always know their own—at least not in the sense of rigid ecclesial bonds. The catholic church (emphasis on the small C) does, however, know its own. Those people who give truthful witnesses to God, of which martyrdom is but one, are recognized by others whose forms of life display continual participation in the life of the triune God. The church remains visible, and this visibility takes place across divisional and geographical lines. The visible church is important not just so the elect can know each other, but because God has promised not to leave the world without a witness to God. The visible church exists for the world as a gift to the world so that the world might know that it is the world. Only then can the world envision for itself an alternative that recognizes the need for repentance, which is the gift of martyrdom.[71] This is the sort of gift that exposes false cities from the true city in an effort to bring all cities under the rule of Christ. The navigation of secular cities (cities rooted in time) is the theme of my next chapter.

4

City: Enduring Enoch

They [disciples] *do not belong to the world, just as I do not belong to the world. Sanctify them in the truth; your word is truth. As you have sent me into the world, so I have sent them into the world.*

—Jesus of Nazareth (John 17:16-18)

At first glance, the above statement appears rather odd. Followers of Jesus are not to belong to this world but they must be in it. That disciples of Jesus are "in the world yet not of it" suggests that Christians maintain an alien-like status in the world (the early Christians were actually called the "third race"). Peter affirms this in his first epistle (2:11), and it is precisely this position of being an alien that I want to examine.

In this chapter, I will consider positioning the Christian as an alien (or stranger/foreigner) in relation to earthly citizenship. That many of us claim, or are required to claim, citizenship within a particular nation-state while simultaneously claiming citizenship in heaven (Phil 3:20) gives us a dual sense of citizenship. Although we retain a localized citizenship on earth, our heavenly citizenship requires that our primary allegiance belongs to the triune God. This does not necessitate disdainful or apathetic practices toward the earthly city; rather, as I will argue, it makes the heavenly citizen subordinate to the nations.

We should not take this to mean that good citizenship is based on support of any and whatever activities our particular nation-state undertakes, but that good citizenship occurs when our lives serve as reminders of who God is. As Christians our mission to make disciples of every nation (Matt 28:19) is *for* the nations, and that is how we are good citizens of both cities.[1] Precisely in being for the nations, however, Christians (as a people) cannot allow their witness to be subsumed by their status as earthly citizens. If we are to be truly for the nations, we must accept the command to be the church. This requires that we take seriously our status as strangers in a foreign land.

It will, therefore, be necessary to flesh out what it means to be a people who are not of the world yet in the world. In Augustinian language, what does it mean to be a people who are on pilgrimage to the heavenly city, yet must do so only through the temporal cities that constitute the world? To be specific, how do Christians simultaneously seek the peace of the city (Jer 29:7) while not forsaking their identity as God's people? By addressing these questions, I intend to show that the Christian allegiance to the heavenly city presumes an exilic posture that confers a missionary stance—a stance that many times takes the shape of martyrdom.

I will do this by first examining Augustine's account of the analogical relationship between the city of God and the earthly city, and how the latter is based on fratricide. That the Christian's dual citizenship is, on one hand, based on an ontology of peace (heavenly) and, on the other, on the rejection of *this* peace (earthly) is crucial to understanding what it means to be a citizen of two cities.[2] Locating one's ultimate citizenship will determine which kind of peace one embodies.

Second, drawing on the recent work of William T. Cavanaugh, I suggest that the birth of the nation-state transforms into a parody the analogy used to negotiate the differences between the two cities. Cavanaugh argues that the earthly city, in the form of the nation-state, attempts to mirror and replace the body of Christ, presenting a rival soteriology to Christianity.[3] If his claim is true, I will need to show why Christianity must neither forget nor neglect its missionary vocation to reveal the victory of the slaughtered Lamb. *How* one seeks the peace of the earthly city will determine the visibility of the kind of witness Christians are called to bear.

In the third section of this chapter, I will use the work of Mennonite theologian John Howard Yoder to further articulate Augustine's claim that Christians are a people on pilgrimage through the world. By using Yoder's work, I give an Anabaptist reading for how Christians, as citizens of multiple cities, might seek the welfare of temporal cities without polluting the ontological transformation Paul speaks of when he claims that we are new creatures in Christ (2 Cor 5:17). By this I intend to explore what it means for Christians to be Christians (new creatures) in a world in rebellion against the Creator of both new and old creatures. That is, how do Christians perform Christianity both seeking the peace of the temporal city and giving witness to the heavenly city?

Finally, I conclude with John's vision, experienced during his expulsion to the island of Patmos. As a Christian who suffered exile rather than martyrdom, he offers a way of seeing the world from the vantage point of the slaughtered Lamb. His particular vision makes possible the kind of eschatological citizenship required to live as a citizen of heaven while here on earth.

Citizens of Everywhere and Nowhere:
The Lineage of Abel

For the ends sought by the civitas terrena *are not merely limited, finite goods, they are those finite goods regarded without "referral" to the infinite good, and in consequence, they are unconditionally* bad *ends.*
—John Milbank

No theologian has articulated in such fine detail the tension between earthly and heavenly citizenship better than Augustine. In *The City of God*, he addressed the reality of the church's location among the worldly cities. He went to great lengths to deliver a historical and practical account of the earthly city, its estrangement from God, and how the church persists through the temporal city.

Augustine noted a basic tension between earthly and heavenly citizenship. This tension, he argued, can be traced back to the sons of Adam and Eve: Cain and Abel. He suggested that citizens of each city could sketch their lineage back to one of these two brothers. Those who belong to the eternal city are descendants of Abel, and those who belong to the earthly city are descendants of Cain.[4]

The very foundation of the first city, Augustine reminded his readers, was predicated on the punishing of a murderer. Its first founder, Cain, murdered his own brother Abel. This, argued Augustine, reflected Cain's own concerns with temporal existence and showed him to be a citizen of the world, while Abel "was pilgrim and stranger in the world, belonging as he did to the City of God."[5]

Augustine interprets this story to be the symbolic beginning of the two cities. The very invention of the city, or at least its caricatured version found on earth, originates from one who seeks a permanent place outside heaven. The descendants of this one, Cain, share with him the desire to live according to human standards as opposed to those, like Abel, who desire to live according to God's will.[6] Abel is the "spiritual father" of the faithful pilgrims on earth, and their practices, including persecution, are forms of participation in Abel's dedication to God (along with the persecution that often frequent such dedication). The persecution itself serves as a reminder that, while life on earth can be good (as creation is good), for the pilgrims of this world, life escapes fruition because life in the city cannot embody the highest good. Whatever peace the pilgrim may find in the temporal city, it cannot lead to union with God, because such peace remains in bondage to time. Life in the city is, according to Augustine, "a life of captivity."[7]

This, however, does not demand either a pessimistic or a dismissive attitude when it comes to the present life for Christians. As citizens of the heavenly city, Christians do not hesitate to obey the laws of the earthly city as such obedience can promote harmony between the two cities. Augustine claimed that the heavenly city "calls out citizens from all nations and so collects a society of aliens" that neither annuls nor abolishes the law of the earthly city. "Rather, she maintains them and follows them . . . *provided that no hindrance* is presented thereby to the religion which teaches that the one supreme and true God is to be worshipped."[8] In other words, Augustine argued that insofar as the earthly city does not interfere with or become an obstacle to the church's practices, the Christian should not rebel against it. He spelled this out in further detail because he knew there is no escape from the city of Enoch. Acknowledging that the church must coexist with the earthly city he argued that as

> long as the two cities are intermingled we also make use of the peace of Babylon—although the People of God is by faith set free from Babylon, so that in the meantime they are only pilgrims in the midst of her. That is why the Apostle instructs the Church to pray for the kings of that city and those in high positions, adding these words: "that we may lead a quiet and peaceful life with all devotion and love." And when the prophet Jeremiah predicted to the ancient People of God the coming captivity, and bade them, by God's inspiration, to go obediently to Babylon, serving God even by their patient endurance, he added his own advice that prayers should be offered to Babylon, "because in her peace is your peace"—meaning, of course, the temporal peace of the meantime, which is shared by good and bad alike.[9]

Augustine picks up the Jeremian posture that the elect cease looking for a permanent home within the world. Instead, they are to seek the peace of the city as a witness to the Creator of all cities.

That God's people are to seek the peace of the city assumes that the city, despite its origins, is not evil. The earthly city is good (it exists only under the providence of God) and is beneficial for both the citizens of heaven and earth. It is, however, not the highest good. Not only is it not the highest good, but it can also exercise the power to lead its citizens to replace the highest good for lesser goods. This, for Augustine, leads to corrupt desires.

Augustine's basic premise is that two conflicting economies of desire work within the world: love of self (*amor sui*) and love of God (*amor dei*). The former love represents the character of the earthly city, while the latter love is encompassed in the heavenly city and is located within the heavenly city on pilgrimage in the world: the church.[10] He said:

> The two cities were created by two kinds of love: the earthly city was created by self-love reaching the point of contempt for God, the Heavenly City by the love of God carried as far as contempt of self. In fact, the earthly city glories in itself, the Heavenly City glories in the Lord. The former looks for glory from men, the latter finds its highest glory in God. . . . The earthly lifts up its head in its own glory, the Heavenly City says to its God: "My glory; you lift up my head." In the former, the lust for domination lords it over its princes as over the nations it subjugates; in the other both those in authority and those subject to them serve one another in love. . . . The one city loves its own strength shown in its powerful leaders; the other says to its God, "I will love you, my Lord, my strength."[11]

The earthly city, though it exists only because of God's providence, nevertheless is a city in rebellion against God. It considers earthly and temporal goods to be *the* good and, therefore, exists as if God does not exist.

If the purpose of the city is to maintain peace, as Augustine suggested, then it is understood as God's instrument. It serves the temporal good by maintaining order against disorder. The church shares this desire for order, yet the church does not hold it as the highest good. Augustine argued that the church uses earthly and temporal things "like a pilgrim in a foreign land, who does not let himself be taken in by them or distracted from his course towards God, but rather treats them as supports which help him more easily to bear the burdens of 'the corruptible body which weighs heavy on the soul.'"[12] Christians may make use of the goods of this world but not in such a way that we become inappropriately attached to them. If this were to happen, such goods would cease to be good, as the attachment would produce a disordered love. Inasmuch as peace and order work for the good of the pilgrim, they are considered useful. The pilgrim can rejoice in such peace as well as in other temporal goods like friendship, health, and romantic love.

These goods, however, are to be rejoiced in only because they serve the goal of the pilgrim: union with the triune God. The only good that is enjoyed for its own sake is God. All other goods are good only because they reflect some aspect of *the* good. Temporal goods serve as analogies to eternal goods and should thereby be used temporally.[13] If the search for such peace distracts the pilgrim from her mission (making disciples of all nations), peace becomes demonic. Ephemeral goods are not worthy of the pilgrim's life, though they do serve as analogical referents to the goods within the city of God. Peace and order within this world are goods, and inasmuch as the earthly city attempts to maintain these goods, it is possible to speak analogically about the two cities.

Graham Ward suggests that terms like *love*, *justice*, and *peace* are predicates of the *civitas terrena*, signifying their parasitic predication on the *civitas dei*. These terms only find "their true significance in relation to Christian eschatology. It is a significance which subverts (or restores) their meaning in the *civitas terrena*."[14] Ward argues that the use of such terminology, as is prevalent in any regime, is only possible given what these terms mean eschatologically. The language belongs to the created order, yet we reside in a disrupted order teetering on the edge of nothingness. He claims that the "perverse imitation" of the earthly city is the "result of the fall when living onto God (*amor dei*) became living for oneself (*amor sui*)."[15] This imitation assumes a god-like positioning by which the living for oneself (and this is the edge of nothingness) is possible by the forgetting of our true love: God.

Our analogical speech about the two cities in the twenty-first century will differ significantly from what was said in the fifth. The temptation to assume a progression from Rome to the United States may entice the Christian to imagine a more "heavenly" earthly city than is warranted. After all, it seems that citizens of liberal, democratic, capitalist regimes experience more freedom, more tolerance, and more luxury than people in the time of Augustine. Whether this is true (and what one means by freedom, tolerance, and luxury would have to be carefully nuanced) is not at stake. However, because many of us do assume some form of progression, we are tempted to allow the nation-state to forget its status as an analogical reference to the heavenly city and to assume the form of the heavenly city. That is, rather than imagining that the earthly city can be good because it exists in reference to the heavenly city, the earthly city assumes a form similar to the heavenly city on earth: the church. As I will argue in the next section, the earthly cities of today—nation-states—offer soteriologies counter to that of the church. They seek to mirror the body of Christ by creating its own myths about human existence, corruption, and redemption and offering a counter-narrative to Christianity.

The Fruition of Cain: The Modern Nation-State

Nothingness, the gods of the nations.
—Regina Schwartz (on Ps 96:5)

In "The City" William Cavanaugh argues that the nation-state is a simulacrum of the church.[16] The body of the state, claims Cavanaugh, is a perversion of the body of Christ. Though the state may be a "false copy" of the church, the danger of its parasitic nature is real. He suggests that inasmuch as the earthly city, now manifest in the structure of the modern nation-state, attempts to "save" humankind from the divisions that plague it, the nation-state is best understood as "an alternative soteriology to that of the Church."[17] It is in this sense that the analogy that Augustine made in reference to the two cities becomes parodic.

Cavanaugh begins his essay by reminding his readers that political theory is characterized by mythology. By this he means that political theory constructs certain myths or stories about the *telos* of life. He claims that the modern state is "founded on certain stories of nature and human nature, the origins of human conflict, and the remedies for such conflict in the enactment of the state itself."[18] The state attempts to remedy the causes of conflict and strife in hopes of bringing humans together for certain common purposes. It does this by giving equal legitimacy to each person, thereby creating the category of "individual" that the state therein serves to protect. The particular *mythos* employed here is that "human government is not based on some primal unity, but from an assumption of the essential individuality of the human race."[19] Cavanaugh maintains that such a story is a crucial element of Rousseau's, Locke's, and Hobbes's political philosophies, because when they suggest that humanity is "born free," what they mean is that humans are primarily free from one another. Such a story runs counter to the Christian narrative, which understands the condition of true human freedom as participation with God and God's creation.[20]

Contractual relations thus replace participatory accounts of the good in many Enlightenment political philosophies. If the state of nature is one of unadulterated individuality, individuals can and must come together on the basis of a social contract. Each individual enters relations with others based on one's own volition and how such a relationship protects both oneself and one's property. This inscribes a now unquestioned distinction between "mine and thine."[21] Humans exercise total control of their property, as if what their property is for has no connection to shared notions of the common good. This serves to sever the individual from any local bodies, like the church, that might lay charge over one's goods or body.

The atomization of citizenry that is so endemic to modern nation-states leaves its citizens, both Christian and non-Christian, without resistance to the myths the state projects. The state creates "the individual," which means that any rights individuals claim (against other people, institutions, or even the state itself) must be negotiated by that which endowed individuals with rights in the first place: the state. Categories such as "human rights" can be useful when employed to protect humans from particular abuses, yet, even in such cases, the use of rights language glorifies the salvific nature of the state —the state is always called on to intervene in human-rights abuses (even against itself). The creation of individuals with natural rights, therefore, serves not so much human agents as it does the state. Once this occurs, there can be no mediating bodies between the individual and the state. To paraphrase Hobbes, the individual answers directly to Leviathan.

Such atomization, argues Cavanaugh, results directly from the state's desire to eradicate difference as a means of achieving peace. Competing individuals cannot come together if their allegiance to other social bodies conflicts with the contractual "polis." Therefore, if unity within the state is to be achieved, the particular and the local must be annihilated (or at least subsumed) to make room for a more "benevolent" universalism.

Cavanaugh points out that state mythmakers such as Rousseau, Hobbes, and Locke were not so naïve to think that the particular could be easily overcome. Those people who imagine that their particular faith actually matters are not going to simply allow their lives to be consumed by the state. The project of the state, therefore, must become the shared project of the many different people who populate a particular geographical location. The creation of civil religion is of particular importance for these thinkers, given that Christianity, inasmuch as it purports to be a body that transcends state boundaries, is a great deterrent to the unifying role of the state.[22] Cavanaugh takes the time to distinguish how each of these three thinkers attempted to deal with the church and discovers that despite their specific differences they agree on one thing: "the need to domesticate the Body of Christ in order to produce unity."[23] The domestication of the church is best accomplished by convincing it to relinquish bodily practices for the more suitable "inward experience."

Christianity must take on a more private or "spiritual" role for the state to place its claims on the body. Salvation deteriorates into the merely personal, and the state becomes the owner of the Christian's body.

The state's usurpation of the role of the church breeds myriad problems for the Christian pilgrim. Most Christians are not ready simply to concede the church to the state, so the next best option, it seems, is a merger of the two. Such a fusion—one that arguably begins with the Edict of Milan, finds fruition in Theodosius's requirement that all citizens (of the earthly city) be baptized and, finally, takes on a truly odd form with the separation of church and state despite Christians governing the state—blurs the line between allegiances to the two cities in that it allows the two to be more easily identified with each other. This identity of the two cities "means that there is no one Church, but exactly as many Churches as there are states."[24] The church becomes divided at the expense of the totalizing nature of the Leviathan. Christianity truly becomes civil because faith becomes a means of binding the individual to the state. The church, as a political body, is eliminated by accepting its designated role as the keeper of spirituality. Its focus now is purely internal—on the soul—while the state exercises free access to the body.[25] Cavanaugh claims that the great "victory" of the state over the church occurs with Locke's principle of toleration of all religion. All religions are to be tolerated, provided that they remain private affairs (that is, are not practiced publicly), which eliminates the church body "as a rival to the state body by redefining religion as a purely internal matter, an affair of the soul and not of the body."[26] Graham Ward agrees with Cavanaugh when he argues that for too long

> the church has viewed itself as looking after the souls or the moral consciences of citizens, and in doing this has handed the very bodies of these citizens over to the secularizing disciplines outside its liturgies, sacraments and walls. For too long church-going has been a private, solitary affair and the church has colluded in finding a position within the city as a guardian of the inner values, the spiritual values.[27]

The church, according to the state, must sacrifice its transnational nature to serve the welfare of the city. Is this, however, what it means to seek the welfare of the city? Must the church give up the body of its citizens in order to serve the state?[28] Only if the state is salvific should the Christian turn her body over to it.[29]

John Milbank opposes the usurped role of the church by the state and claims that our true mother—God and the heavenly Jerusalem—descends in

> compassion for the salvation of the world. Salvation from sin must mean "liberation" from political, economic and psychic *dominium*, and therefore from all structures belonging to the *saeculum*, or temporal interval between the fall and the final return of Christ. This salvation takes the form of a different inauguration of a different kind of community. Whereas the *civitas terrene* inherits its power from the conqueror of a fraternal rival, the "city of God on pilgrimage through this world" founds itself not in a succession of power, but upon the memory of the murdered brother, Abel slain by Cain.[30]

The state, however, fails to enact any true soteriology. It attempts to unify humankind perversely. Its very formation betrays a latent form of atheism that assumes creatures cannot participate in God or in each other. To reiterate, individual rights must be constructed to protect one from others under the power that gives such rights legitimacy: the state. Cavanaugh notes that the myth underwriting the creation of the nation-state begins with an anthropology of equal individuals without common ends. Therefore, the "best the state can hope to do is to keep these individuals from interfering with one another's rights. While this can serve to mitigate the conflicting effects of individualism, it cannot hope to enact a truly social process."[31]

A "truly social process" for Augustine would be rooted in the practice of charity based on love of God, neighbor, and oneself.[32] Only where the triune God is worshipped can there be true sociality. The reunification of the human race for Augustine (and Cavanaugh) depends not on the ability of the state to rally its "people" under fictitious accounts of human embodiment, but on Christians taking seriously their *true* citizenship. The Christian conception of heavenly citizenship for both of these theologians is not an attempt to escape into "otherworldliness," but is rather a "radical interruption by the Church of the false politics of the earthly city. . . . The earthly city is not a true *res publica* because there can be no justice and no common weal where God is not truly worshipped."[33]

No one knows for sure how Augustine might respond to the advent of the nation-state. Though one can imagine that his overall response would not differ significantly from his treatment of the two cities (that is, no matter how thoroughly paganized a city is, Christians must still seek its peace), we have to ask the question of how such a peace is sought. Despite Augustine's rich analysis of the church's predicament in the earthly city, he fails to present the same rich ecclesiology that answers how Christians are to seek the peace of the city in such a way that they do not become the city. It seems that too much is conceded to the temporal city, for how can a pilgrim church be, as in Augustine's time, an imperial church?[34] Therefore the Christian allegiance to the heavenly city is a posture: to be a stranger in a foreign land is the way God would have us be in the world. Such a posture needs to be sketched.

Galuth: Exile as Mission

How could we sing the LORD's *song in a foreign land?*
—Psalm 137:4

In a letter written to the exiles in Babylon, the prophet Jeremiah instructs the Hebrews to build houses, plant gardens, and marry—all within the confines of their diasporic existence. More importantly, Jeremiah demands that they "seek the welfare of the city" and to pray to the Lord on its behalf (29:7). He concludes that the welfare of the city has a direct bearing on the welfare of its inhabitants: citizen and noncitizen alike.[35] This, of course, does not mean that the existence of the Jews, as a people, is dependent upon the earthly city; rather, it points to Augustine's claim that the temporal good of earthly peace is a good.

It would be a mistake, however, to suggest that Jeremiah's command to seek the peace or welfare of the city is little more than this basic observation. To seek the welfare of the city as the holy, elect, and chosen people of God is a mission. The very posture itself—an exilic body of people making their homes in a foreign land—is a socially embodied witness. Exile is the means by which God would have us evangelize the world.

Mennonite theologian John Howard Yoder understood this missionary posture as the hermeneutical key for understanding the Christian's place in the earthly city.[36] To be God's people is to be foreigners in a strange land who, nevertheless, seek the peace of the city. Yoder articulates what this looks like in a way that Augustine failed to do. As Gerald Schlabach argues, Augustine's last word on how residents of the heavenly city should live amid the earthly city "has served Christian traditions in the West not so much as a final answer to the question of how they should order their politics within the passing societies of the age, but rather as a definitive statement of that question." Schlabach concludes that Yoder represents, possibly, the best answer (albeit a late one) to the very question Augustine did so much to sharpen but ultimately left hanging: *how* do Christians seek the peace of the city without losing their identity, and why does this "how" matter?[37]

Yoder argued that that Christians' sense of homelessness in this world stems from the story of Israel. He claimed that Israel's experience with trying kingship and even empire, followed by their ultimate abandonment of them, "is part of the lesson of the biblical witness; exile and the abandoning of nationhood as the form of peoplehood are prophetically interpreted as the way of JHWH. Ezra and Nehemiah reestablish the community precisely *without* national sovereignty."[38] What is most relevant about understanding the Jews as a people without a nation is that there is no paradigm in the Old Testament that suggests how to gain sovereignty or destroy current social orders; instead, the model of how to live under a pagan oppressor is most pressing within the Old Testament narratives. The way of diaspora is the prevalent paradigm for God's holy "nation." As Yoder put it, "To be scattered is not a hiatus, after which normalcy will resume. From Jeremiah's time on . . . dispersion shall be the calling of the Jewish faith community."[39] Yoder continued:

> The move to Babylon was not a two-generation parenthesis, after which the Davidic or Solomonic project was supposed to take up again where it had left off. It was rather the beginning, under a firm, fresh prophetic mandate, of a new phase of the Mosaic project.[40]

In Yoder's estimation, this "new phase of the Mosaic project" is the model adopted by the early church and has continued to be the model for two millennia of rabbinic Judaism.[41]

Commenting on Jeremiah 29, Yoder argued that there are several examples of how the Jews sought the welfare of the city. Not only is there Jeremiah's advice on how to live in exile following the defeat of Josiah, but there are also the similar stances of Joseph in Egypt, Daniel under Nebuchadnezzar, Mordecai in Persia, and in some sense Jonah in Nineveh.[42] Yoder claimed that this suggests a stance that has as its goal not the overthrow of the reigning social order but the positioning of the faithful to be a transformative resource for the social order. The faithful achieve this by revealing to the pagan order that its self-mythologizing religious claims are subservient to the God of Abraham. Yoder stated that the

> Joseph/Daniel/Mordecai model is so characteristic in the Hebrew Bible that we have to claim that this kind of elite contribution to the reforming of the existing order is more often the fitting contribution to the pagan community than any theocratic takeover. The complement to the Exodus of the counter-community is not a *coup d'etat* by the righteous oppressed, but rather the saving message of the resident minority.[43]

For Yoder, such a saving message is compromised whenever God's people imagine that they must grasp power in their respective geographical placements. Such grasping indicates a desire to control history, but God's pilgrims know that history is outside of their control. Both Joseph and Daniel found themselves in the center of idolatrous empires, where it seemed likely that they were either going to have to forsake faithfulness to God or face death. Neither Joseph nor Daniel compromised his faith in an attempt to gain power to exert influence. Instead, both remained true to who they were and to whom they belonged. Both were saved by divine intervention with the attendant result that the pagan tyrants were converted to the one true God.[44]

Such stories teach us that the very placement of God's people as strangers in a foreign land is mission-based. These narratives convey the subversive idea that conversion occurs, lives are saved, and history moves by the miraculous intervention of God. A betrayal of this truth occurs when the people of God understand their scattering in a pejorative manner. The scattering of God's people is the way that God would have us be in the world. How the resident minority "saves" the powers-that-be, therefore, is not by deposing or gaining power (that is, finding a permanent home) but by recognizing the gift it is to be "a confessing community which is viable without or against the force of the state, and does not glorify that power structure even by the effort to topple it."[45]

That God requires God's people to eschew political sovereignty by embodying a different form of politics—one that requires total dependence on God—suggests that the people of God assume a homeless stance within the world. Though we often make our home in the city, we do not make the city our home. Jeremiah's demand that the Jews are to seek the peace of the city is made in the context of other prophets falsely claiming that they will soon inhabit their own land. For the diasporic, those of whom *galuth* is both a judgment and a calling, every land is already a homeland, just as every homeland is also a foreign land.[46]

The theological vision of exile that derives from Jeremiah and the early church is Yoder's vision of what it means not to be in charge. To be in exile means that one is never in a position to rule; instead, one lives without power, trusting wholly in God for daily sustenance.[47] That Yoder understood such a posture to have carried through to the early Christian communities is crucial to his argument. The continuity between Jeremiah's proclamation and the formation of the early church is a hermeneutical key to understanding what it means to be God's people in and for the world.

For Yoder, the "resident alien" is not positioned against the world. Rather, it is *for* the world. Exile does not mean withdrawal. Instead, it gives the church a chance to recognize that history is moved not by kings, emperors, or presidents, but by God. In such recognition, the church is liberated from the world's Babylonian schemes of immortality and fascism to be a witness to the triune God. By embracing her own politic, the church "comes out" of the earthly city, so as not to participate in its sins (Rev 18:4), and seeks its peace by offering it the true commonwealth based on love of God.[48]

Yoder's church (Mennonite) differs substantially, on the whole, from Catholic and Protestant churches in that his Anabaptist tradition does not assume the necessity of adopting the accoutrements of the empire. That emperors need to become Christian or that Christians need to become emperors for the church to accomplish its task is not only mistaken, it is a betrayal of the church's posture. This does not mean that emperors cannot be converted; indeed, the conversion of those "in charge" is the desire of the church.[49] Yet to what do emperors convert if the church merely mirrors the state? If the church is to be true to its specific vocation, the making of disciples of all nations, then it must practice her own politics rather than adopt the politics of those that surround her. To seek the peace of the city is to make citizens of all nations citizens of the heavenly Jerusalem, for the church is convinced that this is both the destiny and desire of creation. In this sense (and this is not necessarily Yoder's claim), it seems that the church, as God's people sent to evangelize the temporal city of Enoch, knows Enoch's desires better than Enoch.

It is for this reason that the church, for Yoder, is not incidental to the world's salvation. It plays the primary role (as a graced vocation from God) in God's bringing of creation into union with God.[50] Such a role serves not only those who constitute ecclesial membership but also those who remain outside such membership. This is what it means for the church to be for the nations. Only if the church is the church can the world even recognize that it is the world.[51] When Yoder claims that the "church precedes the world epistemologically," he is suggesting that the category of world does not even function without the church's narration of such a category.[52] Such language can arise only within a particular grammatical framework that takes seriously its own form of life. Though the church recognizes the obligation of the state to serve God by "encouraging the good and restraining evil," the church never subordinates its role to that of the state.[53] This means not only that the church does not compromise itself in relation to the state, but also that it does not gain its identity either as a reaction against the state or based on its contribution to the state. As Cavanaugh contends, the church is anarchical inasmuch as she is formed continually through the Eucharist, not the state.[54]

Such an argument always runs the risk of being challenged as sectarian or irrelevant. That is to say that if one's identity is not somehow primarily shaped by the state or if one engages in practices that are counter to state-identity shaping processes, then often the assumption is that one has withdrawn from the public sphere—the so-called sphere in which relevancy and politics occur. Yet it is precisely when the Christian recognizes her status as a noncitizen of the earthly city that she becomes most relevant.

Yoder noted that when Jeremiah told the exiles to seek the peace of the city "there was never reason for debate about whether that shalom was knowable to the Babylonians, or about whether it was relevant. The need was for the Jewish exiles themselves to believe that that was their mission."[55] Yoder also suggested that Jonah's reason for fleeing from his mission was not that he thought it sectarian, irrelevant, or imperialistic, but that he actually believed that the Ninevites would hear the word and repent. We are told that not only did the entire city repent, but that the king arose from his throne, disrobed, and covered his body with sackcloth (Jon 3:6). Holding the earthly city accountable to God is hardly a strategy for withdrawal.

For Yoder, the early church—being constituted by messianic Jews— assumed this particular means of existence (exilic) as its calling. He stated:

> Jesus' impact in the first century added more and deeper authentically Jewish reasons, and reinforced and further validated the already expressed Jewish reasons, for the already well established ethos of not being in charge and not considering any local state structure to be the primary bearer of the movement of history.[56]

Following the prophetic line of Jeremiah, Jesus solidified the notion that powerlessness and diaspora are normative for the elect. Diaspora is a graced vocation that, at least until the heavenly Jerusalem descends upon earth, may be the primary posture of Christian vocation.[57] To go out into all the nations, drawing disciples from all earthly cities that they may be citizens of the heavenly city, is the task of the Christian pilgrim (Matt 28:19). By taking this task seriously, Christians participate in the triune God.

Participation in God leads to beatification, and beatification is true citizenship.[58] In a very real way, the church is the polis. The church becomes that place on earth where Christians bodily locate their membership. It is in the church that the heavenly citizen is trained for what it means to be a citizen of the heavenly Jerusalem as well as a citizen for the world. On the other hand, the church is not a polis, because the church does not necessarily occupy a space so much as it endures through time. John Milbank argues that, because of the church's revolutionizing of space, the city of God is a paradox. It is a "nomad city" without walls or gates:

> It is not, like Rome, an asylum constituted by the "protection" offered by a dominating class over a dominated, in the face of an external enemy. This form of refuge is, in fact, but a dim archetype of the real refuge provided by the Church, which is the forgiveness of sins. Instead of a "peace" achieved through the abandonment of the losers, the subordination of potential rivals and resistance to enemies, the Church provides a genuine peace by its memory of all victims, its equal concern for all its citizens and its self-exposed offering of reconciliation to enemies. The peace within the city walls opposing the "chaos" without, is, in fact, no peace at all compared with a peace coterminous with all Being whatsoever. *Space is revolutionized: it can no longer be defended, and even the barbarians can only respect the sanctuary of the Basilica.*[59]

The city of God manifest as the church on earth revolutionizes space by enduring through others' space. It exists as an exiled pilgrim from its true home who, nevertheless, seeks the welfare of those that surround it. This is the gift that God gives to the world: to provide the world with a witness to the true God and God's true city (Matt 24:14).

The New City

O People of God, for wherever ye roam,
Your road leads through the world to eternity, home.

—Stephan Zweig

Peter wrote that, according to the promise of Jesus, "we wait for new heavens and a new earth, where righteousness is at home" (2 Pet 3:13). John, in his revelation, concurred: "Then I saw a new heaven and a new earth; for the first heaven and the first earth had passed away, and the sea was no more. And I saw the holy city, Jerusalem, coming down out of heaven from God, prepared as a bride adorned for her husband" (Rev 21:1-2). John articulated his vision further as he noted that there is no temple in the city, for the Lord God Almighty, the Lamb, is the temple:

> And the city has no need of sun or moon to shine on it, for the glory of God is its light, and its lamp is the Lamb. The nations will walk by its light, and the kings of the earth will bring their glory into it. Its gates will never be shut by day—and there will be no night there. People will bring into it the glory and the honor of the nations. But nothing unclean will enter it, nor anyone who practices abomination or falsehood, but only those who are written in the Lamb's book of life. (Rev 21:23-27)

This city, where night no longer exists, represents the reconciling of all earthly cities to itself where righteous citizens of all nations find completion (Rev 22:2).

Though the pilgrimage finds fruition within the gates of the heavenly city, such space remains elusive. Paul Fiddes points out that the "space" of this city subverts normative accounts of what constitutes a city. The heavenly city is also a temple (Rev 21:22), a paradisal garden (22:2), a chariot-throne of God (4:2-8; Ezek 1:4-28), and more importantly, a person: the New Jerusalem is also the wife of the Lamb (Rev 21:2, 9; 22:17).[60]

After the end of our earthly pilgrimage, Christians do not merely reside in a new city; rather, Christians inhabit a new sociality. Christians "dwell in the Bride."[61] This new sociality demands that we not envision the city as some reality to be observed, for this city is fully participatory. For instance, God's throne is mentioned as the source of life, yet nowhere can it be located. The city merges with the presence of God, and all the inhabitants of the city partake in the divine economy that is the triune God (2 Pet 1:3-4).[62] Fiddes argues:

> This city invites participation in a divine communion of life, promising a fullness of presence that we cannot experience now, but not promising that we shall ever possess God as an object of our desire. There will remain a delightful, enticing hiddenness which elicits and requires engagement in the movements of love. Moreover, this city, unlike a temple, is an image of busy activity and creativity as well as fellowship. So the gates of this city are open, promising that there will be journeys to be made, adventures to be had, strangers to be welcomed and homecomings to be enjoyed. This is no static eternity, no simultaneity, but a healing of time.[63]

Space is not the only thing revolutionized in the heavenly city, for within these gates even time is healed. The healing of time, which is the end of time, does not, however, suggest an end to activity; rather, the perpetual participation in the "divine communion of life" results in a constant "engagement in the movements of love." The heavenly city is a bustling city, for it is within this city that true communion exists.

Christians, being a privileged people privy to such knowledge, reveal to the world such a revelation by being in the world as the world was meant to be and one day will become. Christians are to live eschatologically: we live in the present cognizant of what God has done in the past and will do in the future. By enacting the politics that is the church, Christians provide a glimpse of the new Jerusalem as it will one day come out of heaven. The exiled John, who recorded this revelation for us, claimed that he heard a loud voice coming from the throne of the city:

> See, the home of God is among mortals. He will dwell with them; they will be his peoples, and God himself will be with them; he will wipe every tear from their eyes. Death will be no more; mourning and crying and pain will be no more, for the first things have passed away. (Rev 21:3-4)

In this city, God lives with God's people and because of this there is no more pain, suffering, or death. As a previous vision of God's kingdom foretells in Isaiah 11, there will be no harm or destruction within God's "holy mountain" for the simple reason that the "earth will be full of the knowledge of the Lord" (v. 9). Though this kingdom, this mountain, this city, is not yet fully here, it has come in the person of Jesus, and Christians, by being witnesses to this Jew from Nazareth, are called to give a glimpse of the visions described in both Isaiah and Revelation. How else will the world know them? Without a body of people living eschatologically, how will the world understand such a vision? It is by living within the eschatological parameters of this kind of space and this kind of time (the kind of space within heaven where there are no geographical boundaries and the kind of time in which time is completed, thus giving us all the time in the world) that enables us to live, and to have the patience necessary to live, as peaceable pilgrims who must endure and seek the peace of the earthly cities that surround us.

Paul states in Ephesians 2:19 that we are no longer strangers and aliens but "citizens with the saints and also members of God's household." To belong to God's household is true citizenship. This is citizenship that is not an end in itself but exists for all nations so that they too might enjoy eternal residency in the city of God. This is a citizenship based on pilgrimage and is mission oriented. It is the kind of citizenship that is, as Yoder claimed, genuinely *for* the nations. It is for the nations, for it does not desire to allow the world to continue to exist in rebellion against God. It is a citizenship that calls the sinner out of disobedience. That is to say, it is a prophetic earthly citizenship because it is an eschatological heavenly citizenship.

5

Biography: Oscar Romero

A martyrdom has its own strong light, which says more than a thousand words about life and faith.

—Jon Sobrino

I end this book with the biography of Archbishop Oscar Romero because theology risks being vacant if it is not clear as to what it should actually "look like." By describing the life and death of Romero, I hope that my argument will show itself. In this regard, one might say that the word *martyr* is interchangeable with the word *argument*. That is, Romero, as a martyr, was also an argument. Such correlation of terms rejects modernity's bifurcation of belief and action, and perhaps politics and *religio*—therein reopening the space necessary for understanding why martyrdom is not only an intelligible argument for the existence of God but also simultaneously a critique of the principalities and powers that would execute such an "argument."

That I have chosen to highlight Romero as an argument for my argument that martyrdom is that kind of political act that narrates the world as the world (and exposes the pseudo-politics at work in the world), does not imply that Romero would agree with all that I have said (though, hopefully, there would be much empathy).[1] However, his martyrdom does, as Jon Sobrino states, say more about life and faith far better than anyone can accomplish in an academic work. By examining his life and death, perhaps there can be not only some illumination as to what it means to be a citizen of heaven seeking the peace of the city, but also an understanding of citizenship that is both prophetic and apocalyptic.

Adopting Romero as my quintessential martyr/argument is difficult. As I write, he has yet to be named a canonical martyr. Though this may seem insignificant to some (as the people of El Salvador hardly need Rome to tell them he is a martyr), it is vital to keep in mind that martyrs are martyrs only because the church names them as such. Of course, the laity in El Salvador is the church, yet it remains important to remember that his death has for various ideological and theological reasons yet to be considered an 'official' martyrdom. Romero was accused, both during and after his lifetime, of having been duped by "communist" and/or "leftist" priests, some of whom allegedly defended guerrilla tactics to fight against government-funded oppression. Romero's death, so goes the argument, occurred not because of the assassin's hatred of the faith, but because Romero was manipulated by and aligned himself with a politically suspect way of thinking, which prompted his murder.[2]

I intend to show that Romero handled well the problems inherent with both sides of the fight in El Salvador and aligned himself with neither the right nor the left but with what he understood to be a gospel imperative. In doing so, he did not buy into the politics of any temporal political order, but rather acted on the politics of his church. For this reason I find his noncanonical status as a martyr helpful because it displays a church hierarchy that, in many ways, continues to perpetuate the same kind of thinking about the "political" that made the sixteenth century possible.[3] In this sense, the church universal tends to fail to recognize that it is a politic that should never find itself without people like Romero.

In this chapter I will give a brief overview of Romero's life as it developed and culminated into his time as archbishop. I will then discuss how his tenure as archbishop necessitated his death and how his death, because of the life he lived, is only intelligible in light of the Eucharist. I will conclude by placing his Eucharistic life in the context of the purple crown. Romero's "biography as theology" will, I hope, grant a rich understanding of the possibilities of seeking the peace of the city.

Sentir con la Iglesia

Persecution is something necessary in the church. Do you know why?
Because the truth is always persecuted. Jesus Christ said it: "If they
have persecuted me they will also persecute you."

—Oscar Romero

Archbishop Oscar Romero was killed on March 24, 1980, for his obstinate refusal to bow to the oppression of his people. This oppression was
at least a century old: in 1881 a decision to abolish indigenous communal land rights "stole," for lack of a better word, land from peasants to
enable various coffee magnates to monopolize and consolidate their
holdings. This process of "land theft" persisted for the next fifty years,
when in 1932 an uprising of the native peasants challenged those who
protected the coffee barons: the Salvadoran military.[4] Unfortunately, an
all-out massacre resulted in which more than thirty thousand people
were killed in less than a month.

The "uprising" had other significant consequences in that it granted
unadulterated permission to the government to stop any revolution of any
sort by any means necessary. From then on, any protest against the
nation's politics was viewed as subversive. To even hint at the notion of
sharing land, or any goods for that matter, was decidedly "communistic."
Such appeals were demonized by newspapers as well as the radio and tel-
evision networks—all various forms of media owned and manipulated by
the elite. By 1980, an estimated 65 percent of all peasants were landless,
with less than 2 percent of the Salvadoran population owning the majority of fertile land. Such was the socio-political climate that birthed, and
eventually killed, Oscar Romero.

Born on August 15, 1917, in Ciudad Barrios, a small village on the
eastern side of El Salvador, Oscar Arnulfo Romero left home only thir-
teen years later to prepare for the priesthood. By the age of twenty, he
had left his home country to study theology in Rome, where he was
ordained a priest five years later. He returned to El Salvador the following year, 1943, to serve his people, which he did for almost two and a
half decades. During this time he was highly regarded as a skillful
preacher, was the secretary of the San Miguel diocese, a high school
chaplain, and widely known for his writing in the diocese newspaper.

In 1967 Romero was named the secretary-general of the Salvadoran
Bishops Conference. This change required that he move to San Salvador.

Because he was so well liked, many of his friends and parishioners begged that he not go (and even signed petitions to keep him). Nevertheless, Romero left his position as a priest (a powerfully influential priest) and immediately moved into a seminary in San Salvador. There he was known as something of a "bookworm" who worked diligently—much to the bishops' delight. By May of 1968 Romero's meticulous work paid off, as he became the executive secretary of the Central American Bishops' Secretariat.

Romero's rise in ecclesial power continued at a rapid pace. Within two years of his appointment as executive secretary, the nuncio (the pope's official representative) asked Romero to be an auxiliary bishop under the express wishes of Archbishop Luis Chavez y Gonzalez. Romero wavered but eventually accepted. On June 21, 1970, his ordination as bishop was grandly celebrated, although not by everyone. Many were happy neither with his naming as bishop nor with what they considered to be a rather extravagant affair in light of the abject poverty that so many people faced throughout the country.[5] How could the church justify such a gratuitous use of money when so many of their own were dying of hunger and disease? What kind of bishop would Romero be if he allowed his ordination to be such a grand affair filled with powerful and rich people while those who were supposedly under his care were constantly being oppressed by the upper echelon?

One of the major reasons Romero faced opposition, in light of his naming as bishop as well as his eventual naming as archbishop, was his reaction to both Vatican Council II (1962-1965) and the heavily influential Latin American bishops' assembly at Medellin in 1968. Romero always respected the decisions made at Vatican II and had no intentions of either ignoring or rejecting the direction in which council sent the church. He did not, however, always agree with the conclusions drawn by others concerning how Vatican II's direction should be implemented or with their visions of how a post-Vatican II church should look. In this regard, he was considered quite conservative and no real threat to the status quo (the same traits that eventually led to his naming as archbishop).

The conference at Medellin was truly a landmark in Latin American theology. The work of liberation theologians like Gustavo Gutierrez, Juan Luis Segundo, and Jon Sobrino betray some of the more radical implications of this period. Following Vatican II, this conference, and the theology that grew out of it, declared its commitment against any force that did not decry systemic injustice against the poor. This was a church that was going to be for the poor and the oppressed. No longer would it simply serve as spiritual chaplain to the rich and powerful, but it would place itself on the side of those who were exploited by the elite.

This conference was not simply about giving lip service to the poor, it was an attempt to provide a different way of looking at the world: through the eyes of the poor. Scripture would be read from the perspective of the oppressed, and justice would be sought according to their needs. This was not just a way of thinking concerned with certain ends; rather, this conference made possible an entirely different hermeneutical lens. Such a hermeneutic would have radical consequences as it proceeded to interpret the world from the bottom up.[6]

Such "revolutionary" thinking frightened many in the church, for it was thought that it would only produce more violent confrontations. Initially, this was Romero's concern. He thought that the church should move slowly and carefully. Romero continually warned his people to be wary of "temporal liberation" because true liberation could occur only via baptism into Christ's family. This was not something that liberation theologies disagreed with per se; they simply argued that such liberation must entail some sort of seeking of justice on earth. What was being argued over was how best to seek "the peace of the city." Unfortunately, many of those on the "right" refused to upset certain powerful church members targeted as objects of the new hermeneutical eye, while some on the "left" opted for, or at least sympathized with, guerilla-like tactics to attempt to secure what they understood to be divine justice.

Such forms of what I would call "securing," not "seeking," the peace of the city only resulted in a repetitive cycle of violence that justified both sides' retaliatory behavior. This plagued Romero and, even after his so-called "conversion," he never displayed preference to any group that attempted to procure justice through violence. On this point Romero remained consistent throughout his brief tenure as archbishop.[7]

On February 22, 1977, Oscar Romero was named archbishop of San Salvador. His naming created two divergent emotional climates among the people. On one side were those who were gravely disappointed. They thought that his being named archbishop would only further the oppressive system because he would not pose any challenge to the systemic oppression that was killing poor Salvadorans, but would even stifle the progress created by Archbishop Chavez. On the other side was ecstatic joy—for the same reasons previously listed. Romero had lived a pious life, yet one bred of a quiet intelligence respected by many of his fellow bishops as well as military and government officials. He seemed an unlikely candidate for disrupting their tightly controlled world. To solidify things even further, four days later another Romero, General Carlos Humberto Romero (no kinship biologically), was named minister of defense. For those benefiting from the systematic injustices plaguing El Salvador, his naming was another ringing endorsement of the status quo. The church and the state, so thought many, were safe from any radical interpretations of the gospel that would upset the present balance.

"Be a Patriot, Kill a Priest!"

Despite the fact that Romero represented a victory for those who manipulated much of El Salvador's resources, the church continued to be a thorn in the country's flesh. In 1977, fourteen families owned some 60 percent of farmable land, and many priests refused to be silent about such hoarding and exploitation. One such priest was Rutilio Grande—a good friend of Romero, despite theological differences. Grande vehemently protested monopolization and the exploitation of the Salvadoran people. He publicly denounced the upper-class ownership of the majority of fertile land, which forced the poor to live in almost inhabitable regions. Such denunciations did not go unnoticed, because the criticized families were under the protection of a judicial system and a military that directly benefited from these conditions. To speak out against such injustice was, and always is, dangerous. Father Grande, however, had baptized far too many children who would eventually perish of malnutrition to simply ignore the abuses of power.[8] For Grande, to be a priest was to accept the possibility that, in revealing Jesus, one must be open to the consequences such a revelation brings. This was simply part of any Christian's vocation. Only one month prior to his own death, Grande stated:

> It was a matter of being or not being faithful to the mission of Jesus here and now. And for being faithful there would be reprisals, calumnies, blows, torture, kidnappings, bombs, and if one was an outsiders, expulsion. . . . It is dangerous to be a Christian in our milieu! . . . precisely because the world which surrounds us is founded radically on an established disorder before which the mere proclamation of the Gospel is subversive.[9]

Though he served in a culture that was predominantly "Christian," the "mere proclamation of the Gospel" was subversive. Any Christian who took the gospel at its word and sought to be prophetic in speech or action was considered insubordinate and was dealt with accordingly.

Unfortunately, not only wealthy government officials opposed priests like Grande. Some bishops also opposed his "radical" tirades. After bending to hierarchical pressure, Grande resigned from a position he had held for almost a decade at the seminary in San Salvador (director of social action projects) and became a pastor in Aguilares.

The change in climate did not stifle his spirit but only kindled it, because he spent even more time working and living with his flock. On February 13, 1977, Grande preached what Robert Ellsberg appropriately calls "the sermon of his life." This sermon ensured his eventual place among the martyrs:

> I'm quite aware that very soon the Bible and the gospel won't be allowed to cross our borders. We'll get only the bindings, because all the pages are subversive. And I think that if Jesus himself came across the border at Chalatenango, they wouldn't let him in. They would accuse the Man-God, the prototype of man, or being a rabble-rouser, a foreign Jew, one who confused the people with exotic and foreign ideas, ideas against democracy—that is, against the wealthy minority, the clan of Cains! Brothers, without any doubt, they would crucify him again. And God forbid that I be one of the crucifiers![10]

Grande was accepting the repercussions of his familial heritage: his lineage would descend from Abel, not Cain.

Prior to this point, priests had suffered exile and various forms of abuse, yet an attempted assassination seemed unthinkable. Such a sentiment quickly faded. On March 12, not even two months after Romero's election to archbishop, Rutilio Grande, along with an elderly man and a young boy, were shot to death on their way to celebrate the mass. At the urgings of Romero, an official investigation was promised, though unsurprisingly no clues as to the identity of the assassins were uncovered.

Though Romero had not been blind to the polarity between the rich and the poor, after Grande's death it was as if a veil had been lifted from his face. He began to see clearly what was occurring and how the indifference of the rich to the plight of the poor was nothing short of wicked. At the funeral he told the overflowing mass of people that from Grande's death there was a message "for all of us on pilgrimage."[11] In true martyr fashion, Grande would not be silenced. His death would continue to reveal the gospel and expose all things at odds with it. Grande still spoke, because his death was an act of *imitatio Christi* that would inspire and renew a people who continued to make their journey on the way to the heavenly kingdom.

Sobrino claims that the death of Grande served as a catalyst to the conversion of Romero.[12] Perhaps it was not so much a conversion as a discovery of vocation. Maybe it was something like Paul's experience on the road to Damascus, where he did not undergo a conversion as much as he simply understood Jesus to be the fulfillment of his deeply held faith—and henceforth Paul acted accordingly.[13] Or perhaps, when he was gazing at the body of Grande, Romero felt what Ignatius felt when he was on the road to his martyrdom: that his discipleship had finally started. Whatever it was, a conversion experience, a calling, or an epiphany, Romero became privy to a different kind of vision—one he may have always entertained yet never knew how to fulfill. The murder of Grande enabled him to see things differently. Through the life and death of Grande, Romero came to a better understanding of Jesus. He acquired a different vision, and with this change in vision came a different way of being. One can act in a world that one can see, and Romero had found a different world in which to act.[14]

Following Grande's death, Romero came to life. At the funeral he dismissed all pursuits of justice if they lacked genuine faith. He reminded his people that love, not hatred or vengeance, is the root of the church. He excommunicated the murderers of Grande and his two companions yet hoped for their repentance:

> We want to tell you murderous brothers, that we love you and that we ask of God repentance for your hearts, because the church is not able to hate, it has no enemies. Its only enemies are those who want to declare themselves so. But the church loves them and dies like Christ: "Father, forgive them, they know not what they do."[15]

Romero did not seek revenge, for that is not the way of Christ. Instead, he sought the conversion of murderers, for that is the "vengeance of the Christian."[16]

Romero immediately wrote to President Molina, demanding a thorough investigation. The archbishop even stated that the church would not participate in any act of governmental service unless such an investigation occurred. Romero then led his church into two momentous decisions: first, the closing of Catholic schools for a few days in order to reflect on recent events, and second, a single mass for the following Sunday. It was this latter action that solidified the direction in which this once quiet bookworm was going to lead his people.

The single mass, though opposed by the nuncio, as well as members of the upper class, occurred as an act to display unity and solidarity among God's people as well as to show that the church was no longer going to sit idly by while the principalities and powers destroyed her people. More than one hundred thousand people were in attendance—hanging on every word uttered by the man who orchestrated this single mass. The clergy and the laity had discovered that this archbishop, much to everyone's surprise, was going to be the one who marked a return of the church after her rather long absence.[17]

Due to his arguments with the nuncio, as well as the fact that the Salvadoran government had its own ambassador reporting to the Vatican, Romero thought it wise to make a trip to Rome to clarify to Pope Paul VI the things that had been occurring in his land. Romero explained in detail the human-rights abuses of the government, the monopoly certain families maintained over the land, the dire poverty that so many of the pope's people were suffering, as well as the obstinate response to the church's call to justice—particularly the number of "disappeared" people as well as those known to be either expelled, tortured, and/or slain. To all of this the pope, in reply, took Romero's hands and simply said, "Courage! You are the one in charge!"[18]

Reinvigorated by the pope's support, Romero initiated a relentless attack against injustices in El Salvador. Through the pulpit, radio, letters, private conversations, and public addresses, he demanded that his Salvadoran brothers and sisters treat one another as the very image of God all people present:

> We learn to see the face of Christ—the face of Christ that also is the face of a suffering human being, the face of the crucified, the face of the poor, the face of a saint, and the face of every person—and we love each one with the criteria with which we will all be judged: "I was hungry and you gave me food to eat."[19]

Romero was very specific about how one learns to see the image of God in each person by telling people exactly where to look:

> The face of Christ is among the sacks and baskets of the farmworker; the face of Christ is among those who are tortured and mistreated in the prisons; the face of Christ is dying of hunger in the children who have nothing to eat; the face of Christ is in the poor who ask the church for their voice to be heard. How can the church deny this request when it is Christ who is telling us to speak for him?[20]

The *imago Dei*, clearly shown in the God-man Jesus, is also vivid in those who share in the sufferings of the world.

Romero's words gained a following with the clergy and the poor laity yet disturbed the families and officials of the upper tier. To be sure, things were not always so cut-and-dried. The oppressed were not the only ones feeling the pangs of persecution. "Leftist" groups, such as the Popular Liberation Forces (perhaps a guerilla outfit more than a leftist organization), often performed acts that not only undermined their own causes (such as kidnapping public officials), but gave validity to conservative accusations that, because certain priests sympathized with such organizations, the church was breeding and inciting communistic terrorism. Despite the fact that some groups committed seditious acts because of their concern for the oppressed (and their argument pled self-defense), Romero consistently denounced their violence and any sympathizers with such violence: "Let us not forget. We are a pilgrim church, exposed to misunderstanding, to persecution; but a church that walks peacefully because we carry within us the force of love."[21] The church, because it takes the shape of a pilgrim people on a journey to the heavenly city, does not employ the vices of the earthly city. It shuns them in order to bear witness to the true *res publica*: the city of God.

Romero's peaceable politic was ignored with dire repercussions. The tension peaked when the foreign minister Mauricio Borgonovo was kidnapped and eventually found dead. First a priest is assassinated, and now a high-ranking government official. At the funeral, Romero did much to console the grieving family members and was also quick to remind those present that the church rejects both violence and communism—as these were accusations leveled at it. Romero's protest against violence and vengeance, however, went unheard. On that same afternoon, retaliation came in spades. Four men shot a fourteen-year-old boy and a young priest named Alfonso Navarro in their parish (prior to breathing his last breath, Navarro forgave his murderers). Romero was forced to preside over yet another funeral. Despite his continued and persistent decrying of violence, capitalism, and communism, Romero and his church were consistently berated for maintaining treasonous doctrine and harboring subversive priests. Soon pamphlets were passed around stating the same thing found painted on city walls: "Be a patriot, kill a priest!"

Romero intensified his invective against the violence practiced by all groups, while also attempting to maintain dialogue with both government officials and those in and outside the church who thought it necessary to use violence as a means of liberation for the people. Romero would later proclaim: "We have never preached violence, except the violence of love. . . . The violence we preach is not the violence of the sword, the violence of hatred. It is the violence of love, of brotherhood, the violence that wills to beat weapons into sickles for work."[22]

Romero's critique of violence and his attempt at dialogue extended beyond his country's borders. He wrote to the president of the United States, Jimmy Carter, to ask him to cease sending military aid to the Salvadoran government because it was being used against its own people (his request was denied).[23]

Despite his efforts to thwart the repression of his people, Romero could not stem the violence. By 1980, there was an average of one thousand deaths per month. He was overwhelmed with both grief and anger. The only thing he knew to do was to continue speaking the truth. He preached against the kind of spirituality that allowed one to have an inward Christian disposition while practicing violence with one's body. He decried this Gnostic spirituality as well as the individualistic piety plaguing his church. Disembodied Christianity, for Romero, was no Christianity at all. He claimed that he had been, along with the rest of the church, duped by a "spiritualized, individualistic education" that teaches one to try to save one's soul and "don't worry about the rest."[24] Such inward piety neglects the outward witness necessitated by the gospel. It disregards the call to being a people who give the world a glimpse of who God is.

The true subversion, argued Romero, was not the church's call to solidarity with the poor, but with those who claimed that this was outside the church's obligation to society. For Romero, the church was not merely that place where hearts were warmed while stomachs went empty; rather, the church must, because Jesus is present in it, embody the gospel—thus revealing the kingdom of God. It was no surprise to Romero, for it was fulfillment of a promise, that such embodiment would receive the same treatment the Master received: persecution.

On March 23, 1980, Romero gave his last Sunday sermon. With no international help coming and with many of his own bishops against him, Romero came forward like David to meet the giant, armed not with stones but with words:

> Brothers: you are part of our own people. You kill your own
> campesino brothers and sisters. And before an order to kill that a

man may give, God's law must prevail that says: Thou shall not kill! No soldier is obliged to obey an order against the law of God. No one has to fulfill an immoral law. It is time to take back your consciences and to obey your consciences rather than the order of sin. The church . . . cannot remain silent before such abomination. . . . In the name of God, and in the name of this suffering people, whose laments rise to heaven each day more tumultuous, I beg you, I beseech you, *I order you in the name of God: Stop the repression!*[25]

Such powerful words, befitting a true prophet, did not slay the giant, but it did draw the lines necessary to force one to either choose the way of Christ or the way of the world. Many were not accustomed to such a stark choice. It was convenient to have Christianity and the resources of the world at one's fingertips. It was also unthinkable that a leader of the church would even hint at the notion that the state was being a stumbling block to her people's salvation. To tell the nation's troops that their orders from their leaders required them to disobey God was to usurp power in a way that could not go unpunished.

The next evening, Romero led a mass in the chapel of a small hospital. The mass was a special occasion for the anniversary of a good friend's deceased mother. The only people in attendance were some nuns, nurses, and a few patients. Many of Romero's friends asked him not to lead the mass, as knowledge of the service was public. He insisted, despite his fear of assassination, that he must hold the service.

His homily was short: it included a lesson from 1 Corinthians 15:20-28, Psalm 23, and John 12:23-26. The Gospel reading was particularly poignant as Romero must have understood better than ever its connotations: "Unless, the grain of wheat falls into the earth and dies, it remains just a single grain; but if it dies, it bears much fruit" (v. 24). After the Gospel reading, he read a passage from Vatican II that discussed eschatology and how our hope for a new earth does not allow us to abandon the pursuit of a just order in the here and now. He concluded with a prayer:

This holy mass, this Eucharist, is an act of faith. With Christian faith we know that at this moment the wheaten host is changed into the body of the Lord, who offered himself for the world's redemption, and in this chalice the wine is transformed into the blood that was the price of salvation. May this body immolated and this blood sacrificed for humans nourish us also, so that we may give our body and blood to suffering and pain—like Christ, not for self, but to teach justice and peace to our people. So let us join together intimately in faith and hope at this moment of prayer.[26]

A moment after his prayer Romero was lying at the base of a large crucifix. Like his savior before him, who asphyxiated on the cross, he gasped for air—his blood ran out of his body like the blood of Christ flowing from the dropped chalice. An assassin had shot Romero from the back of the chapel and fled the scene. The killer(s) escaped, and Romero died moments later in a hospital bed—his veins having collapsed due to lack of blood. He was killed simply because he, as Sobrino aptly put it, believed in God.[27]

Entregado

It had been more than eight hundred years since a Christian became a martyr at the altar. In 1170, Thomas à Becket, also an archbishop, was murdered by four knights of King Henry for maintaining that there was only one authority that demanded total obedience, and it did not belong to the king. Oscar Romero was murdered for similar reasons. Paul is clear that Christians are to be subservient to their respective governing bodies (Rom 13), while Peter is clear that our obedience belongs not to men but to God.[28] Both Paul and Peter, and Becket and Romero, were subservient to their government, yet both denied that it exercised ultimate authority over their lives. Since the church and the state are not synonymous terms, and because both demand allegiance, conflict is inevitable. One cannot obey both church and state when one requires something contrary to the other. For Becket, his ecclesial obedience conflicted with his allegiance to the king in terms of the autonomy of ecclesiastical courts; for Romero, obedience to God left him no choice but to suffer with the poor—a suffering made possible by the state.

One of the most significant aspects of Romero's few years as archbishop was his ability not just to be *with* the poor, but to *be* the poor. I do not mean he was poor just in the economic sense, but in the true spirit of accompaniment: as he drew near to the poor he became poor.[29] By defending the poor, by being a voice to the voiceless, Romero became one of the poor. Just as the poor were abused, just as the poor suffered, just as the poor were persecuted, so was he. This, however, was comforting. This was exactly what Jesus claimed would happen and what Paul said Christians should celebrate. Suffering as such is not a matter of celebration; rather, to take part in the sufferings of Jesus is a true sign that the church is being the church. By being poor, in the sense in which one is on the side of the crucified, Romero was merely sharing in God's promises and simultaneously serving as a witness to the God of these promises.

Romero did not think it enough to simply be poor to be poor; rather, being poor contains its own evangelical rhetoric. When the church claims to be the church of the poor, it is not saying it is "biased and scornful of the rich. Not at all. The message is universal. God wants to save the rich also. But precisely because he wants to save them, he tells them they can't be saved unless they are converted to the Christ who indeed lives among the poor."[30] To be poor, as Christ was poor, is to give a message of good news to the world: you too can be poor.

Of course, this is not intended to romanticize poverty. The poor Christian, though she wants to be on the side of Christ, also desires that her oppressor be on the side of Christ. To be sure, Romero was careful not to offer a theological justification for the oppression of the poor: "Many would like the poor to keep on saying that it is God's will for them to live that way. But it is not God's will for some to have everything and others to have nothing. That cannot be of God."[31] Those who have so much at the expense of others are in need of conversion. Romero was killed because his attempt to convert sinners required an upheaval of the social structures that created the distinction between the rich and the poor. To be among the poor was to call the rich away from their sinful ways, not in order to create a heaven on earth but to provide a glimpse of the kingdom of God. In God's kingdom, goods are shared so that no one need lack anything. Because he was a person thoroughly formed by the Eucharist, for Romero the sharing of goods was not optional.

It is important to note how Romero's status as an *entregado* (a person who gives himself or completely to his people) was created by his liturgical formation. In *Theopolitical Imagination*, William T. Cavanaugh argues that the Eucharist operates as a spatial discipline that not only enables Christians to resist the false catholicity of the state, family, or market, but also enables us to be the kind of people in whom true fellowship is enacted due to our participation in God's gift at the altar. Cavanaugh quotes an excerpt from a homily of Grande's to this effect:

> The Lord gave us . . . a material world for all, without borders.
> . . . "I'll buy half of El Salvador. Look at all my money. That'll
> give me the right to it." . . . No! That's denying God! There is no
> "right" against the masses of the people! A material world for all,
> then, without borders, without frontiers. A common table, with
> broad linens, a table for everybody, like this Eucharist. A chair for
> everybody. And a table setting for everybody. Christ had good
> reason to talk about his kingdom as a meal. He talked about
> meals a lot. And he celebrated one the night before his supreme
> sacrifice. . . . And he said that this was the great memorial of the
> redemption: a table shared in brotherhood, where all have their
> position and place. . . . This is the love of a communion of sisters
> and brothers that smashes and casts to the earth every sort of bar-
> rier and prejudice and that one day will overcome hatred itself.[32]

That Romero ordered only one mass, a funeral mass, to be held the Sunday after Grande's death, explicitly reveals the politics of the Eucharist. He demanded one mass that would tell the world that this meal, over the broken body of Christ and his broken servants, must be an act that breaks down all distinctions within the church that would profane it. It is no small wonder Romero's decision for a single mass was considered so momentous. It disrupted the comfortable separation growing between the members of Christ's own body, which, as Romero knew, was causing the church to be sick.

According to a certain interpretation of Paul, improper consumption of the Eucharist can cause not only illness, but also death (1 Cor 11:30). Perhaps it should be added that *proper* consumption of the sacramental elements can cause death too. Romero is an interesting martyr for reflection, if for no other reason than that he was killed at the altar. The corollary between liturgy and politics, between obedience and death, is immediately solidified in the death of Romero. If the church is a politic, the liturgy is indispensable for its enactment. The world *liturgy* simply means "the work of the people," and this work cannot *not* be political. That Romero's fallen body intermingled with the consecrated elements is a beautiful act that reveals what it means to participate in a eucharistic economy. The church has always claimed, qualifiedly so, that outside participation within the Eucharist, martyrdom is not possible. In the case of Romero, it was not simply his habitual feasting on God that prepared him for martyrdom, though it did; rather, it was the act itself—the very act that made him a possible candidate for martyrdom—that directly led to his death.[33]

Romero seems to have understood the connection between persecution, the Eucharist, and resurrection well. At the funeral of yet another assassinated priest, Rafael Palacio, Romero likened the body and blood of Christ to those dying and those remembering their deaths: "This is what the feasts of our church are like, the blood of martyrdom and the hope of Christianity." For Romero, martyrdom was a sign of faithfulness as well as an act that brought credibility to the church:

> How sad it would be, in a country where such horrible murders are being committed, if there were no priests among the victims! . . . It is the glory of the church to have mixed its blood—the blood of its priests, catechists, and communities—with the massacres of the people, and ever to have borne the mark of persecution.[34]

It is a wonderful thing that the church participates in the suffering of the world, because it is a sign of fidelity to the way of Christ.

Though he never thought himself worthy of the gift of martyrdom, Romero did understand that feeding on the broken body of Christ might require him to give up his own life. His last words, just prior to the bullet shattering his body, were prayerful reflections on what it means to eat at the altar of the church: "May this body immolated and this blood sacrificed for humans nourish us also, so that we may give our body and blood to suffering and pain—like Christ."[35] In the ultimate act of gift exchange, the human-divine exchange in which God is the giver of all gifts, Romero's life would not be lost but gained—as resurrection is the last word in the Christian narrative: "I have frequently been threatened with death. As a Christian, I do not believe in death without resurrection. If they kill me, I will be resurrected in the Salvadoran people."[36] Romero's voice continues to go with the Salvadoran people as he, along with all the other martyrs and persecuted peoples throughout history, continue to cry out: "How long, Lord?" (Ps 94; Rev 6:9-11).

The Purple Crown Revisited

The tyrant dies and his rule ends, the martyr dies and his rule begins.
—Søren Kierkegaard

Just moments after Romero finished his prayer, at the altar he lay on the floor, surrounded by his brothers and sisters in Christ, perhaps waiting to see the realization of the vision that had captivated and strengthened Perpetua some seventeen hundred years earlier:

> I went up and saw a vast expanse of garden, and in the midst a man sitting with white hair, in the dress of a shepherd, a tall man, milking sheep; and round about were many thousands clothed in white. And he raised his head, saw me, and said: "You are welcome, my child." He called me and gave me some of the milk which he was milking and I received it in my joined hands, and ate; and all those standing around said "Amen." At the sound of the word I woke, still savouring something sweet.[37]

Perpetua awoke from her vision, a sweet taste in her mouth, with a stronger resolve to do battle with those that rejected the truth that is Jesus. Romero was not to awake on this side of life, but we can be sure that he now resides with Perpetua in the eternal city of God.

There is a great deal of intentionality in linking the vision of a third-century saint with a twentieth-century martyred archbishop. Lawrence S. Cunningham argues that what makes a saint a saint is a certain kind of *charism* generated by a religious vision that becomes central to one's life and leads others to glimpse such a vision.[38] This vision is a graced vision that enables others to see things otherwise not so easily seen. Mother Teresa, for instance, is not just a saint for others to emulate, but she herself points back to "the little way" of St. Therese of Lisieux as one who helped her see what it means to follow Jesus. In order to ground it in historical legitimacy, the intense activism of the Berrigan brothers (Daniel and Phillip) was often likened back to the Jesuit activities of Elizabethan England.[39] Peter Maurin and Dorothy Day, founders of the Catholic Worker Movement and a great inspiration to many Christians who desire to heed the call to discipleship, were greatly influenced by the visions of Francis of Assisi, Teresa of Avila, Catherine of Siena, and Day's favorite saint, Therese of Lisieux once again. Therese was an interesting choice for both Mother Teresa and Day because she stressed that the path to holiness was to be found in the mundane aspects of our daily activities—hardly as exciting as martyrdom.

I mention the prior paths taken by these Christians in order to display the diachronic political community that is the church. Though Romero may not have been particularly interested in the stories of Perpetua or other early martyrs, he understood that the resurrection of Christ overcame a dichotomy between history and the church: there exists a time of no time between those who have found new life in Christ.[40] Romero stood in continuity with all those of a shared vision who had come before him and will come after him. Just as the early Perpetua set a standard that many Christians who followed her have attempted to emulate, Romero represents a different yet similar kind of martyrdom that arises out of nothing more or nothing less than the desire to be Jesus in the world. What renders their lives, teachings, and deaths intelligible to each other is the vision they shared of following the life, death, and teaching of Christ.

It is often tempting to place a romantic or even a nostalgic spin on the death of a certain person. It is difficult to imagine that Romero's, like Jesus', last moments were pleasant ones (though, had they been, this would not be unusual nor in discontinuity with traditional accounts of martyrdom). Choking on one's own blood or trying to catch a breath is nothing to desire (unless one is masochistic).

This is why the great bishop of the third century, Cyprian, developed the parable of the sower as a source of encouragement for the Christian facing death. The martyr may face terrible pain and suffer unthinkable tortures, Cyprian understood, yet her reward for obedience to Jesus will far outweigh the temporal sufferings endured in this life. Precisely these sufferings enable one to receive the purple crown. The bruises, the beatings, and the blood spilt are symbolized in the purple color of the crown that rests on the head of those who persevere. It is no wonder that there was a general antagonism to wearing the color purple in the early church; it was a sign of pride and haughtiness. It indicated a kind of thinking that imagined royalty as something earned or achieved—even something that one could bestow on oneself or on others. True royalty, true politics, however, cannot be achieved, for it is a gift given and therefore can only be received.

Cyprian himself received this gift. He was brought into direct conflict with the politics of this world because of his status as a Christian. The proconsul Paternus, following orders of "the most sacred Emperors Valerian and Gallienus," demanded a response as to why Cyprian refused to observe Roman piety (a piety that is in many ways like that found in many nation-states, where, as long as lip service is given to some "God," blessings will be conferred upon the nation). Cyprian's response was clear: "I am a Christian and a bishop. I know no other God but the one true God, who made heaven and earth, the sea and all that is in them."[41] For his reply, Cyprian was exiled and eventually recalled to receive the purple crown for his disobedience to the commands of the "most sacred emperors." For the Christian, the color purple gains greatest significance when one accepts one's vocation as a martyr. Therein resides true politics, for what could possibly be more political than the worship of the "one true God"?

Romero, unlike many who were less fortunate, was blessed to die in the company of those whom he had nurtured and by whom he had been nurtured his entire life: his ecclesial family. One of the sisters present at Romero's death recalls her initial thoughts:

> It's strange, I didn't feel afraid. Instead I felt courage and ran immediately to help Monsenor. But seeing the tremendous hemorrhage of blood flowing from his nose, mouth, and ears, and realizing I couldn't do anything, my first reaction was to look in the direction of the main door of the chapel from where the shot had been fired. I wanted to see who had done this, but I didn't see anybody.
> At that point I realized that God had heard Monsenor's prayer. . . . The truth is we all expected that this would happen one day; but we never imagined that anyone would dare commit such a sacrilege and kill him at the very moment he celebrated the Eucharist. If we look at it from the perspective of the people, perhaps it was better that way. Martyrdom is not granted to just any person, but only to those who are worthy of it. Monsenor was a saint, and his whole life was a great witness. So it was a *crowning* prize for him, especially since it happened at the altar.[42]

It is significant that those privy to martyrdom in the present speak in the same terms as those privy to martyrdom in the early church: it is a "crowning" moment for the martyr. The purple crown that adorns the head of the great bishop of the third century, Cyprian, is shared by the great archbishop of the twentieth century, Oscar Romero.

Though Romero was often careful to distinguish between what he thought was a significant difference between politics and faith, I have tried to suggest that Christian faith is already a politic that does not need to become political. Amused over certain accusations leveled against him by both the right and the left, Romero, solidifies this point with his rejoinder: "This week I received accusations from both extremes—from the extreme right, that I am a communist; from the extreme left, that I am joining the right. I am not with the right or with the left."[43] Perhaps we can attribute both sides' confusion to their inability to recognize the bizarre politic that is the gospel; all Romero was trying to do was be faithful to the word he was obligated to give.

For Christians it is not a matter of whether we are going to "get involved" with politics; Christians are already a part of a body politic that is anything but apolitical. To distinguish between the sacred and the secular or the religious and the political is to grant them an autonomous space free of the Christian narrative. Such distinctions assume that as Christians we have our place in the church but as far as the public realm is concerned, Christian convictions must be neutralized in order for a nihilistic narrative to narrate the "real world."

Though Romero might not necessarily agree with my account of the inherent politics of the church, his life obliterated the distinctions among what is political, social, ethical, and religious. He found no arena of life that was not subsumed under the command to follow Jesus.[44] In General Carlos Humberto Romero's order to the troops to kill and Archbishop Oscar Romero's order to the troops not to kill, we find a clash that stems from two different body politics—both demanding unadulterated allegiance. When the latter Romero demanded a halt to the repression, he was not acting out of Marxist or any other pseudo-political sympathies; rather, he was simply doing what a good Christian bishop does: calling his people to conversion. For this reason, he had to be killed.

On the day prior to his death, Archbishop Oscar Romero summed up beautifully in two sentences what I have attempted to suggest over the course of an entire book. In terms of the inherently political nature of being a Christian, he modestly stated, "I have no ambition for power, and so with complete freedom I tell the powerful what is good and what is bad, and I tell any political group what is good and what is bad. That is my duty."[45] This is the kind of politics that is the church. It is the freedom that one finds in being a Christian that does not limit one to the left or right side of an ideology. The Christian stands beyond these parameters of ersatz political thought and pronounces a prophetic word that reveals all sides as parodies of that true polity found in the body of Christ. Perhaps unwittingly Romero made the case for a wonderful kind of Christian anarchism, not out of a historically hostile reaction to the nation-state but because what constitutes the church is nothing other than the Eucharist. By partaking of God, we are liberated from all the various modes of political thought that captivate the fascist, the rebel, the democrat, the Marxist, the socialist, and so on, because we are freed to be what no one else can be to the world: Christians. This is its own politic that does not need to adopt the politics of a secular, supposedly neutral, free space; but by following Jesus one comes into critical engagement with all other political realities precisely because one cannot but engage the world.

Such engagement with the world has often replicated the death of Jesus in his disciples. Indeed, this is an expectation that stems from the conscious desire to follow Jesus. In this sense, martyrdom must be viewed as both a sign of exclusion and a sign of election. Those who are martyred are often so for the protection of a particular civil order. Martyrs are understood to be the kind of threat that undermines the necessary lies needed to sustain the false politics of this world. Paradoxically, just this exclusion from the city (for being put to death is exclusion from the *polis* or *civitas*) makes politics possible. There are no politics without a conception of citizenship, and there is no conception of citizenship without a conception of those who are excluded from citizenship—the noncitizen makes politics possible because she makes citizenship possible.[46]

However, martyrdom is also a sign of election. Martyrs are chosen to die like Jesus that those outside communion with God might see who God is. This is the vengeance of the Christian: that the sinner might be converted. This conversion, however, is dependent upon God first choosing a people to be a light to the nations. As with all forms of election, exclusion is a natural by-product. In this case, however, exclusion is overcome through Jesus. Jesus came first for the Jews and only secondly for the Gentiles. As the election of Israel in the Old Testament makes clear, election comes at the expense of other peoples. Yet this election also offers other peoples the opportunity to be engrafted into the story of Israel. Such engrafting may very well demand the lives of the engrafted.

In the first chapter I drew on Tertullian to initiate the claim that the life of a Christian is lived in direct confrontation with all the principalities and powers that attack the gospel. I quoted *De Corona*, in which Tertullian described one of the emperor's soldiers who had recently undergone a conversion. The soldier was belittled, attacked, and deemed a traitor because he refused to worship the false gods of the world. In so many ways, this anonymous soldier of the second century has much in common with the Latin American Archbishop Oscar Romero. Like the soldier, Romero too was more "steadfast than the rest of his brethren, who had imagined that they could serve two masters."[47] Romero was also targeted or "marked" out, "jeered at" by many, both in and out of the church—all of whom were "gnashing on him near at hand." Romero, like the soldier who came before him some eighteen hundred years earlier, could only reply to his critics as to why he did what he did with, "I am a Christian." For such a reply, his body dropped to the chapel floor "purple-clad with the hope of his own blood."[48]

Epilogue

Gift—A Non-sacrificial Economy

After this I heard what seemed to be a loud voice of a great multitude in heaven, saying, "Hallelujah! Salvation and glory and power to our God, for his judgments are true and just; he has judged the great whore who corrupted the earth with her fornication, and he has avenged on her the blood of his servants."

—John of Patmos (Rev 19:1-2)

Practice resurrection.

—Wendell Berry

In *The Beauty of the Infinite*, David Hart argues that when the church remembers its nature as a kerygmatic suasion, it immediately goes about the business of telling its own story. The church's story is one of peace, and so it engages "in the practice of a persuasion that is also a practice of the peace it proclaims." Hart continues:

> The Christian evangel means to embrace all creation, and so must seek to evoke love from the other, the aesthetic rapture that captivates (or liberates) by its splendor. . . . Christian rhetoric must seek to induce this rapture, this reorientation of vision that lifts one into another order of seeing, that seizes one from oneself.[1]

Hart is aware that such an "inducement" comes "perilously close to the imagery of seduction," as any unapologetic form of persuasion will do. He argues, however, that Christianity can resist the temptations of power if it opts to remain faithful to its own specific form of persuasion:

> Christianity can only return to its understanding of peace, its unique style of rhetoric, as the sole source of accord; it must always obey the form of Christ, its persuasion must always assume the

145

shape of the gift he is, it must practice its rhetoric under the only
aspect it may wear if it is indeed Christian at all: martyrdom.[2]

Christianity must always, if it is to be Christian, take the form of Christ.

One of the most important aspects of martyrdom is that it is an exercise in persuasion. Martyrdom is a form of witness, and to bear witness is always to point to something else beyond the act itself. As Hart rightly argues, martyrdom is a moment in rhetoric. It is an argument for the existence of God. It attempts to persuade and convert others to its story, based on the very structure that it takes. A Christian can tell the story of Christ only by "assuming the shape of the gift" that is Christ. This means that the act of martyrdom is not just a gift given to the recipient, as Christian history has always claimed, but martyrdom is a gift given to the watching world. It is a gift given not just to the faithful community left behind, but to the undecided and even to those who are the reason for the possibility of the reception of the gift. That is, martyrdom is a gift given to the enemy. By taking the form of Christ, the martyr presents the enemy with a first-hand encounter with Christ himself. In this way, martyrs are never, technically speaking, victims; rather, they are, plain enough, martyrs.

Martyrs, Not Victims

Descriptions create imaginative worlds, and the imaginative worlds of a victim and of a martyr are different. A victim is the subject of domination or one who suffers an injustice. This carries with it connotations of tragedy, not in the ancient sense of something fated, but in the more contemporary sense of something sorrowful that should not have occurred and thus hints at senselessness or wont of teleological purpose. Martyrdom is anything but tragic (in either sense of the word).[3] It does not live in a world of tragedy but in a world of apocalypticism.[4] Martyrdom participates in the ongoing creation of not an alternative world but an authentic world: a world inaugurated by the cross and the empty tomb is the world in which the martyr resides. It is a world that is here and is not yet here. It is predicated on hope, as strictly speaking, tragedy must deny. It is a world that is invoked and displayed for all to see by the actions of those who live in it.

In one's reception of the gift of this world, the recipient can do nothing other than share this world with others. That is why the Christian must always find herself on the side of the excluded, on the side of the crucified, against those who would crucify. The world of crucifiers is one created and perpetuated by the false myth of an ontology of violence, a world that can know nothing other than violence because that is the way, according to this mythos, "the world is."[5] The only answer to this false ontology is the practice of an ontology of peace, the practice of resurrection. Rejecting the sacrificial logic of this pagan story, Christianity answers with the "infinite gesture of Christ's sacrifice."[6]

This is a sacrifice we cannot make or repeat. But it is one in which we can participate. At the most rudimentary level, martyrdom is hardly a sacrifice, for the simple reason that whoever loses her life gains her life. An exchange occurs in which the martyr receives eternal life (according to the early church, such reception is immediate). Resurrection renders martyrdom nonsacrificial. This does not mean that, since Christ is risen, his crucifixion is not a sacrifice, for Christ is not a martyr.[7] The martyr imitates Christ and may die *like* Jesus but not *as* Jesus. There is only one redemptive sacrifice, and ours is not it. The sacrificial logic assumed by the world is one that can be overcome only by another sacrifice, but one that does not merely repeat the same sacrificial logic it opposes. This sacrifice fulfills the created order and undoes the economy of violence at work in the world. This sacrifice does not appease a vengeful God, for this sacrifice is one of gift, not debt.

> In Christ, totality's economy of violence is overcome by the infinity of God's peace, inasmuch as one order of sacrifice is overcome by another: sacrifice as the immolation of the beautiful is displaced by a sacrifice whose offering is one of infinite beauty.[8]

The sacrifice of Christ is the fulfillment of an order based on excessive, never-ending giving.

Hart contends that Christ crucified is a "metahermeneutical." By this he means that Christ crucified is the interpretive "form" by which Christians narrate all other interpretative ideologies. Christ crucified, argues Hart,

> stands outside modernity, outside the market, outside every human order of power, as a real and visible beauty. Nor can worldly power ever overcome him in his mystical body, because, again, the very gesture of the rhetoric of his form is one of donation, of martyrdom, and one that the powers of the world can suppress only through a violence that creates martyrs, and so confirms—contrary to all it intends—the witness of a peace that is infinite. In the time of sin, governed by an eschatological hope that has already been imparted in history but that is still also deferred, Christian rhetoric can be only a declaration of witness, and a gift. A gift of martyrs— which is the name that must, finally, be given to the Christian practice of persuasion—can never be returned violently as the Same; because this gift is always peace and beauty; violence can receive the gift, but never return it. . . . Christians can struggle only by way of martyrdom, by surrendering their gift to others even in the moment of rejection.[9]

Precisely in the moment of rejection, martyrs are at their best because they imitate Christ in his moment of rejection. In this moment of rejection, of a feeling of abandonment that even Jesus weathers, the ultimate gift is given: the redemption of creation through the slaughtered lamb. The martyrs retell this story with their deaths, placing themselves out of any narrative that would call them victims, for they are blessed with the opportunity to participate in the perpetual gift-giving exchange that occurs between God and God's creation. Understood in this vein, martyrdom escapes both criticisms of masochism or misanthropia and inaccurate forms of praise in the terms of altruism or sacrifice. Martyrdom, or Christianity for that matter, is neither altruistic nor sacrificial, for it participates in an economy not of scarcity but of abundance.

A Eucharistic Economy

To each one of us Christ is saying, "If you want your life and mission to be fruitful like mine, do like me. Be converted into a seed that lets itself be buried. Let yourself be killed."

—Oscar Romero

Truth is unkillable.

—Balthasar Hubmaier

Having the willingness to die, to become a martyr, is not easy. It requires participation in an ecclesial body that makes available the communion with God necessary for one to die well—to die in Christ. As I claimed earlier, the Eucharist has always served as a—if not *the*—crucial practice to a life directed toward martyrdom (and in this case I mean "witness" in the broad sense of the word). Lacking this fundamental practice of the church renders difficult the ability not only to produce martyrs but also to provide any understanding of why martyrdom may be necessary. Feeding on (though never consuming) the body of Christ is more than an act of remembrance, more than a foretaste of the heavenly banquet, and it is more than a time of reconciliation and confession of sin. To be sure, it is all of these things, but it is also so much more (this is part of what makes it a sacrament, or a mystery). The Eucharist makes participation in the divine economy possible because it makes particular claims on the participant's bodies. In the physical act of eating and drinking Christ, we commit ourselves to a life like Christ's life.

Whether or not one considers the elements in the Eucharist to be transformed into Christ (though this is an important debate), the implications of what it means to feed on our broken Savior (even if but in a "symbolic" way) remain salient. If one's understanding of Christ's eucharistic presence is symbolic, this nevertheless does not imply that one's discipleship should exist on a symbolic level.[10] A life following Christ is a life like Christ's: it is corporeal. Discipleship, because of its imitation of and participation in the life of Christ, is a matter of ontology. If Christ is both fully human and fully divine, participation in him, along with the participation within the Trinity that the Eucharist makes possible, renders discipleship ontological. To fully be requires a life in Christ.

Athanasius once stated that in order to know Christ, one must follow Christ. If Christians are to avoid the judgment of being liars, we cannot claim to know Christ if we do not follow him (1 John 2:4). To know this person, why we follow him, or why we would even want to follow him, we must remember who he is, what he did, and how these things implicate us in a life like his. For this, the habitual partaking of the Eucharist is crucial. In sharing his life through this meal, we are saved from a disembodied Christianity. Without the Eucharist, Christianity becomes but one more phenomenon predicated on "spirituality." It becomes a matter of "feeling" that sentimentalizes the radical and disruptive nature of Christianity that makes people like Ignatius, Becket, and Romero impossible.

Participation in the Eucharist does not, of course, have to lead to martyrdom (the lives of Dorothy Day, Mother Teresa, and countless others attest to this); it simply makes martyrdom, one specific form of *imitatio Christi*, possible—not only possible, also intelligible, because by participating in the Eucharist we pledge to have our bodies, if necessary, broken.[11] We cannot feed on Christ and not accept the repercussions of such a feeding. As Christ's body was broken for us, ours too may also be broken, if we are to be faithful to the way of Christ. In this sense the Eucharist reorients our entire lives by putting us on the path of the crucified one.

Although I am arguing for the Eucharist as a practice that helps Christians accept the path of the slaughtered Lamb, I do not think that the Eucharist entails a fetishization of death. Neither does it make of tortured death a thing of nostalgia or desire. Christianity is not masochistic. Death is not to be desired, only imitation of Christ is worthy of our desire. Such desire may result in death, but the moment of death is not the moment of longing, for it is the revealing of Jesus in a world hostile to the gospel that is the content of Christian pining. That this has often resulted in death is not proof of a Christian's desire to die but merely evidence that Jesus spoke the truth: "If they persecute me, they will persecute you."

Both life and death are present on the path of the crucified one. The Eucharist recalls both of these realities (if death can, appropriately, be called a reality) and subjects them to the eternal reality that is the triune God. William Cavanaugh argues that any true anthropology, any true theology, must recognize that humans are "made" members of God's own body through the Eucharist. "Just as the living Father sent me, and I live because of the Father, so whoever eats me will live because of me" (John 6:57).[12] We participate in each other because we are created in the image of God. Our feeding on Christ's body places us within the economy of God and gives us the awareness and skills necessary to participate well within the rest of creation. Cavanaugh explains that Christ is not simply at the "center" of the Eucharistic meal or of the church; he resides at the margins, being radically "identified with the least of my brothers and sisters." Cavanaugh continues:

> Christ is the center of the Eucharistic community, but in the economy of the Body of Christ, gift, giver, and recipient are constantly assimilated to one another, such that Christ is what we receive, He who gives it, and "the least" who receives the gift, and we are assimilated to Christ in all three terms.[13]

Romero, Cyprian, Felix Mantz, and all the martyrs through history are part of an economy by which participants are gifts, givers, and recipients, all aesthetically assimilated in the perpetual gift giver, the triune God.

The importance of the Eucharist for a faithful account of martyrdom cannot be overstated. What keeps martyrdom from being sacrificial, from being a tragic event, is its connection to the Eucharist. The Eucharist is an eschatological banquet that promises resurrection based on the one and only redemptive sacrifice possible: Jesus on the cross. The crucified Jesus is, as Hart reminds us, not a debt appeased but a gift freely given. Our offerings at the table, as well as our reception of this gift that is Christ's sacrifice, place us in a gift-exchange economy of pure gratuity. This excessive gratuity is nowhere more clearly displayed than at the altar. In *After Writing*, Catherine Pickstock argues that the reception of the body and blood of Christ in the Eucharist is a reception of

> that which has already been offered to God by Jesus. This confirms that even the receiving of gift is still an offering; that in the liturgy, there is no action outside gift, but only the repetition of the offering which has already been made by God to Himself in the person of Jesus.[14]

For Pickstock, we can do nothing but receive that gift that has already been given—our offering is a reception.

Paradigmatically, the unity of offering and reception in the Eucharist shows that there is nothing we can give to God that has not already been given to us. There is no gift outside God. All our gifts are nonidentical repetitions of God's gifts that enable us to participate in the gift-giving relations that characterize the triune God. Seen in this way, Christ's death is not a gift of a debt paid so much as it is a gift given by which our responses are themselves nonidentical gifts. Hart contends that this gift given by God in Jesus is prior to debt and therefore "prior to any stablilizing economy of violence" which is shown in the resurrection:

> God's balances are not righted by an act of immolation, the debt is not discharged by the destruction of the victim and his transformation into credit; rather God simply continues to give, freely, inexhaustibly, regardless of rejection. God gives and forgives; he fore-gives and gives again. There is no calculable economy in this trinitarian discourse of love, to which creation is graciously admitted. There is only the gift and the restoration of the gift.[15]

To participate in the Eucharist is to prepare for an imitation of Christ on two accounts: first, in his death, and second, in his resurrection. By feasting here on Christ we prepare the transitory nature of our bodies for a "glorified" body—one that is beyond decay and corruption. Part of the gift of the Lord's Supper is that we remember not only the death of Christ but also his resurrection. Hence Balthasar Hubmaier's observation on the person of Jesus (and those who participate in him): "Truth is unkillable."[16]

Vita autem hominis, visio Dei

The greatest sign of faith in a God of life is the witness of those who are willing to give up their own life.

—Oscar Romero

I have not wanted to praise martyrdom at the expense of any other form of witness. Living a life of obedience takes many forms, and not everyone is chosen for the gift of martyrdom. Many live lives of everyday, ordinary (though no less difficult) fidelity to the way of Jesus. Though I am convinced that faithfulness results in a life of anything but "ordinary," it is also the case that feeding the poor and visiting those in prison are examples of faithfulness not easily romanticized. Obedience to Jesus can be mundane and very ugly. Holding the hands of a dying leper in Calcutta contains its own beauty, though I imagine disposing of the limbs that fall off the leper is not a pretty sight. The nun who spends her entire life bathing the unwanted leper and then dies silently in her convent, without making headlines on the nightly news, makes Jesus just as visible as the highly dramatic tortured death of the martyr.

Martyrdom, like any other form of witness, is praiseworthy only because it points to Jesus. It is one act of fidelity alongside many others that displays a person's belief in God. What makes this act so fantastic is its ability to separate the believer from the nonbeliever. In a culture where it takes more conviction to be a pagan than to be a Christian, the acts of the martyrs are wonderful reminders of what is really at stake in Christianity. Even more wonderful are the reflections we must make on the lives lived that lead to the necessity of why martyrs became martyrs. From these narratives we gain wisdom as to what it means to follow Jesus.

The martyr's death mimics the death of Jesus, but only because her life also mimics the life of Jesus.[17] It is not just the dying or "how" one dies that is crucial; rather it is the life lived that makes such a death possible that must be at the center of our thinking. Martyrdom is only a final sign or a confirmation of one's holiness. It is a testament to a life well lived—a life that is blessed to show Christ not only in life but also in death.

The above subtitle, "*Vita autem hominis, visio Dei*," perfectly sums up how we are to think of martyrdom. Irenaeus, in the midst of early church persecution, claimed that the "life of the human being is the vision of God."[18] It is life lived that is the vision of God. It is the way one lives that reveals the truth, goodness, and beauty of our claims. On occasion, such beauty is rejected and affords one the opportunity to continue to reflect the triune God's beauty in the way one dies. Yet this latter moment is only possible because of the life lived that led to this final "earthly" imitation of Christ.

Because they take the gospel at its word, the martyrs provide an illuminating kind of continuity that stems from Stephen and traverses the various lives and deaths of all kinds of Christians throughout history. These Christians all share in common a certain trait described by the author of Hebrews 11:32-39. The author recognizes that there is not enough time to tell "all the stories" of the prophets, kings, and saints that constitutes God's people. There is not enough time to detail how through faith they "conquered kingdoms, administered justice, . . . shut the mouth of lions" (v. 33). There is not enough time to tell of how often they were cut in two, stoned to death, and forced to wear sheep's clothing. Therefore, the author simply asks, "And what more should I say?" The world was not worthy of them."

Notes

Introduction

1. Engin F. Isin, *Being Political: Genealogies of Citizenship* (Minneapolis: University of Minnesota Press, 2002), 1-5.

2. Ibid. As an example Isin discusses slavery: slaves were not just excluded from citizenship (whether in antiquity or in the recent history of the United States) but "made citizenship possible by their very formation" and categorization as slaves (51).

3. Ibid., 4.

4. Given that Christianity drew from all classes, there were martyrs who were citizens and martyrs who were not. However, in their decisions to die as witnesses to the truth that is Christianity, their exclusion from the city rendered their previous status inconsequential.

5. Though the act of withdrawal, whatever that may look like, could be construed as a political stance, I am not clear on how, in any *positive* sense of the word, it would be political unless the intention is to offer an alternative picture of how life outside the polis can alter life inside the polis. Being exiled, or in the case of the martyrs (permanent exile), however, may be more advertently political as those within the polis are declaring their politics over and against those who they deem are bad for the polis.

6. Oliver O'Donovan, *The Desire of the Nations: Rediscovering the Roots of Political Theology* (Cambridge: University of Cambridge Press, 1999), 212.

7. Eusebius, *The History of the Church from Christ to Constantine*, trans. G. A. Williamson, ed. Andrew Louth (London: Penguin Books, 1985), 141.

8. Eusebius, *History of the Church*, 142.

9. *The Epistle to Diognetus*, 5.1-9, trans. Henry G. Meecham (Manchester: Manchester University Press, 1949), 79-80. The writer continued by drawing an analogy between the body and the soul and the Christian and the world. Just as the soul is in the body but not of the body so are Christians in the world but not of the world. Though this is not the place to argue for or against the author's antagonistic dichotomy between the soul and the body, the analogy is useful insofar as it presents a vivid image of what it means to be in the world but not of the world.

10. Augustine wrote during a turbulent period. He was connected to and

remained reliant upon the work of the "early church" (understood to have been the golden age of martyrdom). Yet his work came after the fusion of church and empire, which created a kind of nostalgia for the prior era. Finally, Augustine witnessed the inevitable fall of Rome. All three of these factors combine to shape his account of citizenship.

11. William T. Cavanaugh, "The City: Beyond Secular Parodies," in John Milbank, Catherine Pickstock, and Graham Ward, eds., *Radical Orthodoxy: A New Theology* (London: Routledge, 2000), 185.

12. Augustine, *Concerning the City of God Against the Pagans*, 19.24, trans. Henry Bettenson (London: Penguin Books, 1984), 891.

13. Chris Huebner argues that martyrs live out of control partly because being a martyr means giving up the narration of one's life. A martyr cannot simply say, "I am a martyr," because being a martyr requires a remembering body-politic to do such naming. See "Between Victory and Victimhood: Reflections on Martyrdom and Culture," *Direction: A Mennonite Brethren Forum* 34, no. 2 (Fall 2005).

14. John Howard Yoder, *The Priestly Kingdom: Social Ethics as Gospel* (Notre Dame, IN: University of Notre Dame Press, 1984), 11.

15. I claim here that the church is the bearer of history, whereas Yoder claims that the church is the bearer "of the meaning of history." The difference, if any, is that I am attempting to conflate the two by suggesting that the medium is the message. This is to say that martyrs, both by their very lives and deaths, do not point to some other meaning but are the bearers of meaning, of history, because of their participation and subsequent deification in the triune God.

16. Eusebius, *History of the Church*, 138.

17. Mark Water, ed., *The New Encyclopedia of Christian Martyrs* (Grand Rapids: Baker Books, 2001), title page.

18. The word *martyr* derives from the Greek *mártus*. Initially, *mártus* did not imply death, but meant roughly "one whose knowledge of a specific event was due to being present at it, so that she could give an account of the event." In his *Martyrdom and Rome* (Cambridge: Cambridge University Press, 2002), Gary Bowersock argues that what we now mean by martyrdom, that is, a "blood-witness," is a Christian invention of the mid-second century.

19. Stanley Hauerwas, *With the Grain of the Universe: The Church's Witness and Natural Theology* (Grand Rapids: Brazos Press, 2001), 205-41.

20. In part, this is what Mark Water suggests in his *Encyclopedia of Christian Martyrs*. He begins with Bramley-Moore's comment that "the history of Christian martyrdom is, in fact, the history of Christianity itself" in order to argue that Christianity can be traced, historically, only through its visible witnessing to Jesus (a witnessing that does not have to take the form of blood-witnessing, but still requires a witness). As Water appears to

assume that the highest form of such witnessing is blood-witnessing (a claim substantiated by much of the early church) my argument builds upon this by locating true political activity as that activity that reveals the true politic: the kingdom of God. Martyrdom, in a very real way, conflates the categories of both witnessing and politics.

21. William Cavanaugh describes how, prior to the sixteenth-century, *religio* was understood as a habit, a bodily practice, and a virtue. In this sense, Cavanaugh argues, *religio* should be conceived as a binding obligation that makes possible communion with God. See Cavanaugh, "God is not Religious," in D. Brent Laytham, ed., *God is not . . . Religious, Nice, "One of Us," An American, A Capitalist* (Grand Rapids: Brazos Press, 2004), 97-115. Christianity has always been critical of "spiritualizing" the faith. That Christianity has taken on a more disembodied form after the nineteenth century suggests indebtedness to both Enlightenment liberalism and the second-century heresy Gnosticism—not historical Christianity. For an excellent critique of the modern market's creation of spirituality, as well as its use within a socio-economic order bent on domesticating the practice of *religio*, see Jeremy Carette and Richard King, *Selling Spirituality: The Silent Takeover of Religion* (New York: Routledge, 2005).

22. Jon Sobrino, *Witnesses to the Kingdom: The Martyrs of El Salvador and the Crucified Peoples* (Maryknoll, NY: Orbis Books, 2003), 52.

Chapter 1
Spectacle: The Early Church
1. Ignatius, *Letter to the Romans*, 2 in *Ante-Nicene Fathers* (hereafter *ANF*), ed. Alexander Roberts and James Donaldson (1885; repr. Peabody: Hendrickson Publishers, 1999), 1:74.

2. Ignatius, *Letter to the Romans*, 3 in *ANF*, 1:74. I am indebted to George Kalantzius for teaching me the complexities of Ignatius's desire for martyrdom. Ignatius was a local bishop in Antioch with no universal authority or appeal save that afforded him in his future martyrdom. For him to have abandoned or been saved from martyrdom would have amounted to abandoning all claims to have authority or to act as a mediator in ecclesial disputes. Despite, however, the intrigue of power and authority in the early church, particularly surrounding the martyrs and confessors, I hesitate to assume that this was in the foreground of Ignatius's thought. Flight from persecution was permissible in the early church (save for Tertullian's harsh—though rather astute—invective against flight, Cf. *De Fuge in Persecutione*, in *ANF*, 4:116-25), but escape from persecution belongs in a different category. Fleeing can be understood as an imitation of Christ and a following of his teachings. Clement of Alexandria argues that not to flee makes one an accomplice in the crime of the persecutor. The first task, therefore, of the

Christian is to flee, because Christians do not want their persecutors to commit the sin of murder. Cf. Clement, *The Stromata* 4.10, in *ANF*, 2:423. Escaping, however, seems to be an attempt to avoid the will of God. For a more comprehensive evaluation of the Christian's requirement to either "stand their ground or flee," see O. P. Nicholson's "Flight from Persecution as Imitation of Christ," *JTS* 40 (1989): 48-65.

3. Thieleman J. van Braght, *The Bloody Theater or Martyrs Mirror of the Defenseless Christians*, 2nd English ed., 23rd printing (Scottdale: Herald Press, 2001), 107.

4. Cf. Robin Young, *In Procession Before the World: Martyrdom as Public Liturgy in Early Christianity*. (Milwaukee: Marquette University Press, 2001).

5. This is not to suggest that no martyrs died in isolation or in exile; indeed, many died outside the walls of the arena. Yet, even in those cases, the exile was public knowledge and a political event. Exile was and remains a political act because citizenship gains its intelligibility from those outside the city.

6. Origen, *Exhortation to Martyrdom*, 16 in Origen, *Prayer* and *Exhortation to Martyrdom*, in Johannes Quasten and Joseph C. Plumpe, eds., *Ancient Christian Writers*, 19, trans. John J. O'Meara (Westminster: The Newman Press, 1954). Emphasis is his.

7. Cyprian refers to this contest as the "contest of God, the spiritual contest, the battle of Christ" in which those powers opposed to God manifest their rebellion against God's own. Cyprian, *Epistle 8*, in *ANF*, 5:288.

8. Eusebius, *History of the Church*, 120.

9. Ibid., 121.

10. Joyce E. Salisbury, *Perpetua's Passion: The Death and Memory of a Young Roman Woman* (New York: Routledge, 1997), 126.

11. Cyprian, *Epistle 55*, in *ANF*, 5:347.

12. Cyprian., *Epistle 8*, in *ANF*, 5:288.

13. Tertullian, *The Apology*, 27, in *ANF*, 3:41.

14. Salisbury, *Perpetua's Passion*, 120.

15. Tertullian, *De Spectaculis*, 15, in *ANF*, 3:86.

16. For a more detailed description of the arena see Thomas Wiedemann's *Emperors and Gladiators* (New York: Routledge, 1992).

17. Salisbury, *Perpetua's Passion*, 120.

18. Ibid.

19. Wiedemann, *Emperors and Gladiators*, 46.

20. The suggestion that the word *games* could be interchangeable with *politics* is not unfounded. Salisbury convincingly argues that "private honor and public good intersected in the arena" inasmuch as the games were often sponsored by a generous donor who, though not unconcerned with his or

her own reputation, was concerned about the general welfare of Roman culture. Salisbury, *Perpetua's Passion,* 121. The implication being made here is this: these were not just "games"; they were life.

21. René Girard describes sacrifices such as this as the state's attempt to secure peace and order within its realm. It is not so much the case that Polycarp posed an actual threat to the social order, but that his death was a symbol of the ongoing well-being, and legitimation, of the state. Cf. Girard, *Violence and the Sacred* (New York: Continuum International Publishing Group, 2005). To the contrary, I am suggesting that in a very real sense the martyrs did pose a threat to the state. Insofar as the martyrs represented Christ and their persecutors represented all that is hostile to Christ, then each witness is a threat to that which stands against Christ.

22. Tertullian, *De Spectaculis,* 7, in *ANF,* 3:82.

23. Tertullian, *De Spectaculis,* 26, in *ANF,* 3:90. Tertullian tells the story of a woman who visited the games and came back possessed by a demon. After the demon was exorcised, it was asked why it dared to attack a Christian, and it responded: "I found her in my domain."

24. Rowan Greer, trans. *Origen: An Exhortation to Martyrdom, Prayer, and Selected Works* (New York: Paulist Press, 1979), 42.

25. Lactantius reported a conversation, a century later, between Diocletian and Maximian, in which Diocletian attempted to dissuade Maximian from killing any more Christians precisely because of their ability to find honor and glory in such deaths. *De Mortibus Persecutorum,* ed. and trans. J. L. Creed (Oxford: Clarendon Press, 1984), 19.

26. Eusebius, *History of the Church,* 118.

27. Cyprian, *Epistle 8,* in *ANF,* 5:288.

28. Ibid.

29. Eusebius, *History of the Church,* 142.

30. Cf. Ignatius, *Epistle to the Smyrnaeans,* 3, in *ANF,* 1:86-88.

31. Cf. Ignatius, *Epistle to the Smyrnaeans,* 3; in *ANF,* 1:86-88, as well as Irenaeus, *Against Heresies,* 14; in *ANF,* 1:541-542. For a more comprehensive introduction to the issues at stake against Docetism, see Alister McGrath's *Christian Theology: An Introduction,* 4th ed. (Oxford: Blackwell Publishers, 2007), 281-90.

32. In the epilogue I will discuss in greater detail why it is the case that the death of the Lord's saints escapes the realm of the "tragic."

33. Judith Perkins, *The Suffering Self: Pain and Narrative Representation in the Early Christian Era* (London: Routledge, 1995), 15-40.

34. John Chrysostom, *A Homily on Martyrs,* in Wendy Mayer and Pauline Allen, *John Chrysostom* (London: Routledge, 2000), 94. Chrysostom continues: "Have you imitated a martyr? Have you emulated his virtue? Have you run in the steps of his philosophy?" (94).

35. Young, *In Procession Before the World*, 10.

36. Sources ranging from *The Octavius of Minucius of Felix*, 37, in *ANF*, 4:196, to *Martyrs Mirror* attribute the martyr's ability to endure torture to the presence of God within the believer. Brad Gregory, in his book *Salvation at Stake: Christian Martyrdom in Early Modern Europe* (Cambridge: Harvard University Press, 1999), gives careful consideration to this topic as he suggests that one of the ways the sixteenth-century church attempted to discern the distinction between a true martyr and a false one was based on how they reacted during their torture and death (55, 66, 320).

37. Young, *In Procession Before the World*, 10.

38. *The Epistle Concerning the Martyrdom of Polycarp*, *ANF*, 1:39.

39. Cf. Cyprian, *Epistle 57*, in *ANF*, 5:352-53.

40. Cyprian, *The Writings of Cyprian*, vol. 2, *An Exhortation to Martyrdom*, 52.

41. Cf. Cyprian, *Epistle 55*, in *ANF*, 5:347, where he argues that the Christian, if she is to have any hope of winning the crown awarded in martyrdom, must consume the Eucharist *daily*. Also see Edelhard L. Hummell, *The Concept of Martyrdom According to St. Cyprian of Carthage* (Washington, D.C.: The Catholic University of America Press, 1946), 70-73, for an extensive account of Cyprian's requirements for proper training for martyrdom. It should be noted, however, that many Christians in training— catechumens—were often martyred prior to their full immersion in the church. In these cases, most early church theologians (if not all) argued that their martyrdom constituted the baptism they lacked in their earthly life. Cyprian argues in *Epistle 72*, in *ANF*, 5:385, that martyred catechumens receive the effects of the first baptism. This is not necessarily incongruous with Cyprian's prior argument, because what made their martyrdom possible is the church as well as the Holy Spirit.

42. Young, *In Procession Before the World*, 31.

43. Irenaeus, *Against Heresies*, 4.32.9, in *ANF*, 1:508. Emphasis is mine.

44. Young, *In Procession Before the World*, 33.

45. Ibid., 34-35.

46. Ibid.

47. Cyprian, *The Treatises of Cyprian*, 11, in *ANF*, 5:497.

48. Cf. Cyprian, *On the Glory of Martyrdom*, in *ANF*, 5:585. Cyprian says, "Assuredly God, who cares for all, gave to life a certain medicine as it were in martyrdom, when to some He assigned it on account of their deserving, to others He gave it on account of his mercy. Martyrdom is medicinal because it leads to the death that leads to life."

49. Cyprian, *Treatise 11*, in *ANF*, 5:497.

50. Origen, *Exhortation to Martyrdom*, 171.

51. Mark 10:38. See also Jesus' words on the baptism he had yet to receive in Luke 12:50.

52. Origen, *Exhortation to Martyrdom*, 168.

53. This was the predominant view during the time of Origen's writing. Cyprian in *Exhortation to Martyrdom, Addressed to Fortunatus*; Tertullian in *On the Resurrection of the Flesh*; and Eusebius in his *History of the Church*, bk. 6, make similar arguments.

54. Tertullian, *On Baptism*, 16, in *ANF*, 3:677.

55. Tertullian, *Scorpiace*, 12, in *ANF*, 3:646.

56. Tertullian, *On Baptism*, 16, in *ANF*, 3:677.

57. Tertullian, *On Baptism*, 16, in *ANF*, 3:677.

58. Tertullian, *Scorpiace*, 12, in *ANF*, 3:646.

59. Tertullian, *The Passion of Perpetua and Felicitas*, 6.4, in *ANF*, 3:705. The chant was, of course, a mocking of Saturus, yet it encapsulates for the early Christians their understanding of both baptisms.

60. Tertullian, *Scorpiace*, 9, in *ANF*, 3:649.

61. Cf. Cyprian, *On the Glory of Martyrdom*, in *ANF*, 5:579-87.

62. Edelhard L. Hummell, *The Concept of Martyrdom According to St. Cyprian of Carthage* (Washington, D.C.: The Catholic University of America Press, 1946), 130.

63. Ignatius, *Epistle to the Romans*, 5, in *ANF*, 1:75. I contend, and this will be one of the central arguments of this book, that it may be fair to say that his discipleship begins with living the kind of life that leads one to a conflict with the powers-that-be and ends in its ultimate imitation of Christ. This is, however, the luxury I have of looking back over the life of Ignatius. Nevertheless, Ignatius should be taken at his own word when he says, "Now I begin to be a disciple."

64. Cyprian, *On the Glory of Martyrdom*, in *ANF*, 5:579-80.

65. Cf. Tertullian's comments in 8 and 9 of *Scorpiace*. Clement of Alexandria argues that martyrdom is a perfecting of the Christian life, not because one comes to the end of his or her life, but because the martyr "has exhibited the perfect work of love." (*The Stromata*, 4.4, in *ANF*, 2:411.)

66. In *Martyrdom According to John Chrysostom* (Lewiston, NY: Mellen University Press, 1997), Gus George Christo gives special attention to the manifold effects of martyrdom for the believer in Chrysostom's work. He suggests that for Chrysostom, emigration into heaven, a spiritual wedding between Christ and believer, and an exchange of corruptibility for incorruptibility are some of the powerful effects martyrdom has for the Christian.

67. Tertullian, *On the Resurrection of the Flesh*, 4, in *ANF*, 3:576.

68. Tertullian, *A Treatise on the Soul*, 55, in *ANF*, 3:231. Emphasis is mine.

69. Cyprian, *Epistle 8*, in *ANF*, 5:288.

70. Cyprian, *Epistle 76*, in *ANF*, 5:404.

71. Tertullian, *Apology*, 50, in *ANF*, 3:55.

72. Cyprian, *Epistle 8*, in *ANF*, 5:289.
73. Tertullian, *On Idolatry*, 18, in *ANF*, 3:72-73.
74. Tertullian, *The Chaplet, or De Corona*, 14, in *ANF*, 3:98.
75. Tertullian, *The Chaplet, or De Corona*, 1, in *ANF*, 3:93.

Chapter 2
Body: The Field of Combat

1. Cf. Augustine's *Treatise on the Soul*, 1, where he has to correct popular errors deduced from the *Acts of Perpetua and Felicitas*, which were apparently being read as if they were of canonical status. For a more detailed account see Johannes Quasten's comments in *Patrology*, vol. 1, *The Beginnings of Patristic Literature* (Allen: Christian Classics, 1995), 181.
2. Bruno Chenu, et. al, *The Book of Christian Martyrs*, trans. John Bowden (London: SCM Press, 1990), 70-71.
3. Eusebius, *History of the Church*, 140.
4. Herbert Musurillo, ed., *The Martyrdom of the Saintly Apostle Apollonius, also called Sakkeas* in *The Acts of the Christian Martyrs* (Oxford: Clarendon Press, 1972), 99. Voluntary martyrdom, strictly understood, is that act by which one provokes and seeks death. Such a desire, argues the early church, arises more out of a longing for death than a desire to imitate Christ. Martyrs freely give of their bodies, but they do not ask someone to take it from them.
5. Tertullian, *On the Resurrection of the Flesh*, in *ANF*, 3:551. Tertullian quotes Isaiah 66:23 in defense of this claim: "'All *flesh* will come to bow down before Me,' says the Lord" (567).
6. Cyprian, *Epistle 8*, in *ANF*, 5:288.
7. Harold Bloom, in his book *The American Religion: The Emergence of a Post-Christian Nation* (New York: Simon & Schuster, 1992), argues that Gnosticism, after taking a brief hiatus, has fully recovered in the twentieth century. He argues that it holds the majority of North American faiths captive, rendering specific bodily practices unnecessary.
8. Cyprian, *Epistle 8*, in *ANF*, 5:288.
9. Tertullian, *The Passion of Perpetua and Felicitas*, in *ANF*, 3:705.
10. Eusebius, *History of the Church*, 142.
11. Ibid.
12. Elaine Scarry, *The Body in Pain: The Making and Unmaking of the World* (Oxford: Oxford University Press, 1985), 210-20.
13. Ibid., 204.
14. Ibid., 203.
15. For an accessible account of the gender connotations that stem from using masculine language in reference to God as well as orthodoxy's denial of a "body" to God, see Alister E. McGrath's *Christian Theology: An*

Introduction (Oxford: Blackwell Publishing, 2007), 88-89, 103, 194, 203-5. McGrath is helpful inasmuch as he points to a variety of sources that deal specifically with both the language used in speaking of God and the historical theologians who, despite referring to God as a "he," never assumed that God was male. Of course, language creates worlds, and despite their own best theology that would deny the attributing to sexual organs to God, the continued use of masculine language has, nevertheless, created a god who appears to be male. If this is the case, feminists such as Mary Daly are theologically correct to argue for the castration of such a god. Cf. Daly, *Beyond God the Father: Toward a Philosophy of Women's Liberation* (Boston: Beacon Press, 1985), 71-73.

16. Ibid., 212. Though Jesus does bless those who have not seen yet still believe (John 20:29), such belief remains contingent upon a body of people witnessing to who Jesus is. Despite our inability to see the bodily form of Jesus from Nazareth, the church embodies the life of Jesus so that we can, in a very real way, see Jesus.

17. Ibid.

18. Stanley Hauerwas, *With the Grain of the Universe: The Church's Witness and Natural Theology* (Grand Rapids: Brazos Press, 2001), 205-41.

19. Scarry, *The Body in Pain*, 34.

20. Cf. Peter Brown, *The Body and Society: Men, Women, and Sexual Renunciation in Early Christianity* (New York: Columbia Press, 1988), 323-38.

21. Cf. Patricia Cox Miller, "Desert Asceticism and 'The Body from Nowhere,'" *Journal of Early Christian Studies* 2 (1994), and Benedicta Ward, *The Sayings of the Desert Fathers* (Kalamazoo: Cistercian Publications, 1975), xvii-xxvii.

22. M. Therese Lysaught, "Witnessing Christ in Their Bodies: Martyrs and Ascetics as Doxological Disciples" *The Annual of the Society of Christian Ethics* 20 (2000): 257.

23. Cf. Brent D. Shaw, "Body/Power/Identity: Passions of the Martyrs" *Journal of Early Christian Studies* 4, no. 3 (Fall 1996). See also Michel Foucault, *Discipline and Punish* (New York: Vintage Books, 1995).

24. Teresa M. Shaw, *The Burden of the Flesh: Fasting and Sexuality in Early Christianity* (Minneapolis: Augsburg Fortress Publishers, 1998), 174.

25. Therese Lysaught, "Eucharist as Basic Training: The Body as Nexus of Liturgy and Ethics," in David M. Hammond, ed., *Theology and Lived Christianity* (Mystic, CT: Twenty-Third Publications, 2000), 257.

26. For a more extended account as to how the liturgy shapes Christians in ways counter-cultural to that of the designs of North America see "Liturgy: God Bless America: Public Worship and Civic Religion," ed. by

D. Stephen Long *Journal of The Liturgical Conference*, Vol. 20, Number 1, 2005.

27. Lysaught, "Eucharist as Basic Training," 259. I qualify her notion of the body as the site of resistance (that is, "secondarily") for if it is stated that way, the body colludes with the object of its protest. That is, it becomes defined by that which it is attempting to resist. If this is the case, then the body, it seems, requires persecution in order to fulfill its performative task. Making persecution a necessity for the embodiment of Christianity is problematic. Though Jesus does claim that his followers will be persecuted, like himself, our performance of the Christian life, however, arises not out of response to persecution (at least, primarily) but simply out of obedience.

28. Cf. Paul McParlan, *The Eucharist Makes the Church* (Edinburgh: T&T Clark, 1993). Throughout Christian history the Eucharist and the church have both been referred to as *corpus Christi*.

29. William T. Cavanaugh, *Torture and Eucharist: Theology, Politics and the Body of Christ* (Oxford: Blackwell Press, 1998), 225-26. The forty-nine Abitene martyrs were saying that they could not live without their Eucharistic celebration.

30. Ibid., 268.

31. Maureen A. Tilley, "The Ascetic Body and the (Un)Making of the World of the Martyr," *Journal of the American Academy of Religion* 59, no. 3: 471.

32. Teresa M. Shaw, *The Burden of the Flesh: Fasting and Sexuality in Early Christianity* (Minneapolis: Fortress Press, 1998), 5.

33. Chenu, *Book of Christian Martyrs*, 40.

34. *The Encyclical Epistle of the Church at Symrna: Concerning the Martyrdom of the Holy Polycarp*, 15-16, in *ANF*, 1:42.

35. Lysaught, "Witnessing Christ in Their Bodies," 245.

36. Ibid.

37. *Concerning the Martyrdom of the Holy Polycarp*, in *ANF*, 1:42.

38. Lysaught, "Witnessing Christ in Their Bodies," 246.

39. Eusebius, *Church History*, 5.20.4. Polycarp's flesh is eventually consumed by the fire, but only after his death.

40. Lysaught, "Witnessing Christ in Their Bodies," 249.

41. *Concerning the Martyrdom of the Holy Polycarp*, in *ANF*, 1:42-43.

42. Ignatius, *To the Magnesisans*, in *ANF*, 1:59.

43. Ignatius, *To Polycarp*, in *ANF*, 1:94.

44. Leonard L. Thompson, "The Martyrdom of Polycarp: Death in the Roman Games," *The Journal of Religion* 82 (2002): 39.

45. Tertullian, *The Passion of Perpetua and Felicitas*, in *ANF*, 3:704.

46. Ignatius, *To the Trallians*, in *ANF*, 1:70-71.

47. Ibid.

48. Ignatius, *To the Symrnaeans*, in *ANF*, 1:88.

49. Ibid., 88-89.

50. Justin Martyr, *Fragments of the Lost Work of Justin on the Resurrection*, in *ANF*, 1:297.

51. Ibid.

52. Ibid., 298.

53. Ibid., 297-99.

54. Irenaeus, *Against Heresies*, in *ANF*, 1:528.

55. Ibid.

56. Caroline Walker Bynum, *The Resurrection of the Body in Western Christianity, 200-1336* (New York: Columbia University Press, 1995), 39. Emphasis in original text.

57. Ibid.

58. Ibid., 6. Perhaps the notion of a "spiritual body" is not an oxymoron. Maybe it is just difficult to envision what this looks like given our (post)modern predilection for making disembodiment a prerequisite for being spiritual.

59. Ibid.

60. Ibid.

61. Tertullian, *On the Resurrection of the Flesh*, in *ANF*, 3:584.

62. Ibid.

63. Bynum, *The Resurrection of the Body*, 50.

64. Eusbeius, *Church History*, 148.

65. Tertullian, *A Treatise on the Soul*, in *ANF*, 3:231-35, and *On the Resurrection of the Flesh*, in *ANF*, 3:567-72. Ignatius clearly did not find what occurred to one's body after death to be problematic. He actually hoped that his entire body would be consumed by the beasts so that his fellow Christians would not have to chance being exposed as Christians by having to bury his body. Ignatius, *Epistle to the Romans*, in *ANF*, 1:75.

66. Tertullian, *On the Resurrection of the Flesh*, in *ANF*, 3:567.

67. Felix Minucius, *Octavius*, in *ANF*, 4:194.

68. Ibid.

69. Felix Minucius, *The Octavius of Minucius Felix*, in *ANF*, 4:179.

70. Jesus' flesh seems to take on different characteristics after his resurrection. Graham Ward argues that the "resurrected body of Jesus sums up all the modes of displacement that were seen in evidence before his death." The "unstable physicality" that accompanies the body that walks through doors is countered by a corporeality that is tangible and, for instance, is capable of consuming food. Though his body is not immediately recognizable, it is still a body. Ward suggests that Jesus' resurrected body must be thought of analogically. Just as our bodies move through time and constantly change, these changes "are analogically related to each other." As the unrecognizable body

of Jesus reveals itself to be the resurrected body of Jesus, a new understanding of the body is revealed: the corruptible body will be redeemed in its complete totality. See Graham Ward, "The Displaced Body of Jesus Christ," in *Radical Orthodoxy: A New Theology*, eds. John Milbank, Catherine Pickstock, and Graham Ward (London: Routledge, 1999), 173.

71. Mary Timothy Prokes, FSE, *Toward a Theology of the Body* (Grand Rapids: Eerdmans, 1996), 162. The seed that is sown also bears fruit in the present church. For instance, the image of the seed has never been lost on the martyrs. Tertullian's most famous quote, "The blood of the martyrs is the seed of the church," is recalled in Father Alfred Delp's last letter: "After one thing I strive: to sink into God's earth and into His hand as a fertile, healthy seed." (161) Though the martyrs will be resurrected in heaven they are also resurrected, in a metaphorical way, in the church on earth. Their witness, as it is remembered and named by the church, carries the church on its journey toward the heavenly city.

72. Bynum, *The Resurrection of the Body*, 41.

Chapter 3
Performance: The Sixteenth-Century Debacle

1. Thieleman J. van Braght, *The Bloody Theater or Martyrs Mirror of the Defenseless Christians*, 2nd English ed., 23rd printing (Scottdale: Herald Press, 2001), 442.

2. Ibid.

3. Maureen A. Tilley, *Donatist Martyr Stories: The Church in Conflict in Roman North Africa* (Liverpool: Liverpool University Press, 1996), 45. It seems that the reason for Caecilian's actions was a Roman law prohibiting bringing food to prisoners. Perhaps, therefore, the bishop was thinking about keeping other Christians safe. This, however, may give the situation too charitable an interpretation. Given the nature of historical Christian thought about the self (that is, it is better to die than to preserve oneself or others by avoiding Christian faithfulness), such a notion, that is, that his response was merely an attempt to preserve the lives of other Christians, sounds much more like a modern account of altruism than the standard readiness of many early Christians to die for their convictions. Such a charitable read also denies the legitimacy of the angered and abused voices of these Christians to the physically abusive Caecilian (not to mention his later, lapsed state).

4. Ibid., 45-46.

5. Tilley, *Donatist Martyr Stories*, xvi.

6. The primary sense in which the Donatists could be understood as "purists" was that they descended from martyrs and confessors. That is, their tradition lacked *traditores* (unless they had been sacramentally reinitiated).

Being a Donatist did not immediately imply nonviolence as it would for later so-called purists like the Anabaptists of the sixteenth century (save for a few sporadic first-generation Anabaptists like the Muensterites). To be fair, it may be the case that as many Protestant and Catholics of the sixteenth-century harped on the few violent episodes of early generation Anabaptists (if they can even be properly called Anabaptists) in an attempt to link them all in the same group, perhaps the same can be said for *certain* Donatists or Donatist theology in general. The Christian historian Justo L. Gonzalez is also careful to mention that many Donatists tried to disassociate themselves from the Circumcellions. *The Story of Christianity*, vol. 1, *The Early Church to the Dawn of the Reformation* (SanFrancisco: Harper Collins Publisher, 1984), 156. Unfortunately, it seems that most of what we have to go by in terms of Donatist thinking comes from the opposing/victorious side. This makes it difficult to know whether or not their positions or their practices have been, as Peter Brown suggests, "caricatured." Cf. Brown, *Augustine of Hippo* (Berkeley: University of California Press, 1969), 212-43. Brown gives a very detailed account of Augustine's characterization of the Donatists as he attempted to eliminate this threat to orthodoxy.

7. Cf. Augustine's letter to Emeritus in *The Political Writings of St. Augustine*, ed. Henry Paolucci (Washington, D.C.: Gateway Editions, 1962), 192.

8. W. H. C. Frend, *Martyrdom and Persecution in the Early Church: A Study of Conflict from the Maccabees to Donatus* (Garden City, NY: Anchor Books, 1967), 411. Once again much difficulty arises from statements like this, because even Menno Simons blatantly disapproved of the violent actions of the Donatists. Cf. his "A Pathetic Supplication to all Magistrates," in *The Complete Writings of Menno Simons* (Scottdale: Herald Press, 1956), 525. We should not assume, however, that Simons had any better resources than most when it came to the actual positions and practices of the Donatists.

9. Paolucci, *Political Writings of St. Augustine*, 185.

10. Ibid., 186.

11. For an excellent account of Augustine's justification for governmental coercion against the Donatists, see Peter Brown's chapter *Disciplina* from his biography of Augustine, *Augustine of Hippo*, 233-43.

12. Paolucci, *Political Writings of St. Augustine*, 216.

13. Brown, *Augustine of Hippo*, 241. Brown notes that laws against Donatists became coercive in the "true sense of the word" as people were punished for "*not* becoming Catholics" (334). The lines blur between whether the Donatists were a problem more for the Church or more for the Catholic Empire. Augustine had already opened the doors for the capital punishment of heretics in bk. 1, chap. 21, of his *City of God* where he argues that the imposition of the death penalty on those who are enemies of the state is a legitimate

and obligatory practice of the state. This becomes even more interesting if we ask if his account of predestination did not also serve to further the justification of capital punishment for heretics. In lieu of hearing the news of a Donatist bishop claiming that he will burn down his own church with his people in it if the Catholics do not cease the repression Augustine states: "Seeing that God, by a hidden, though just, disposition, has predestined some to the ultimate penalty (of hellfire), it is doubtless better that an overwhelming majority of the Donatists should have been collected and reabsorbed . . . while a few perish in their own flames. . . ." (336). Augustine seems notably unconcerned with this group as he seems to assume their death, as well as their home in the after-life, is divinely orchestrated as a punishment for their not being Catholics.

14. It is important to note that not all blood spilled was due to the so-called Religious Wars. William T. Cavanaugh astutely argues that the sixteenth century also saw the birth pangs of the nation-state. He reminds us that there were many cases of Catholics killing Catholics and Protestants killing Protestants not in the name of orthodoxy, but in regards to state allegiance. This, of course, plays a crucial role in the subversion of what it means to be political. Part of the burden of this chapter will be to show how a politics of sorts is occurring throughout the killing and dying of this turbulent century, yet it betrays a kind of politics that suggests an "at homeness" in this world rather than the politics of the nomadic pilgrim Christians are called to be. Cf. *Theopolitical Imagination* (London: T & T Clark, 2002).

15. Van Braght, *Martyrs Mirror*, 482.

16. Brag Gregory gives an excellent account of the various means employed by sixteenth-century Christians to argue whose martyrs were genuine. After examining these attempts, Gregory suggests that the notion of correct doctrine was the "end-all" decisive factor. Cf. *Salvation at Stake: Christian Martyrdom in Early Modern Europe* (Cambridge: Harvard University Press, 1999), 315-40.

17. Cf. Stanely Hauerwas's *Sanctify Them in the Truth: Holiness Exemplified* (Nashville: Abingdon Press, 1998), 19-36.

18. Friedrich Nietzsche once remarked that if Christians actually believed what they claimed to believe, they would still be killing heretics, because they lead "legions into eternal damnation." He states, "Not their love of men but the impotence of their love of men keeps the Christians of today from—burning us." Cf. *Beyond Good and Evil: Prelude to a Philosophy of the Future* (New York: Vintage Books, 1989), 84. Such a comment should not be lost on Christians. Nietzsche is pointing out what he thinks to be either a lack of love on the part of Christians or a lack of belief in the claims Christianity makes. Otherwise, issues of doctrinal orthodoxy would still matter. I find this terribly interesting because his insights are so descriptive of the apathy that plagues twenty-first-century Christianity.

19. Cf. Gregory, *Salvation at Stake*, 84-90.

20. I have no reason to doubt this important distinction, though I cannot help but wonder how, and at what cost, it became possible for Christians to prosecute religious deviants in the first place. Such concern is one that underscores the assumption that Christians should be a people "in charge," as if the governing of the world is our primary concern. It is also important to note that Jesus was "prosecuted" in full accordance with the law though he, as well as two thousand years of church tradition following him, seemed to have understood it as persecution. Nevertheless, Gregory's chapter on this distinction is very important and cast the motivation of the "inquisitor" in a more benevolent light. Cf. Gregory, *Salvation at Stake,* 74-96.

21. Water, *The New Encyclopedia of Christian Martyrs*, 745.

22. John Foxe, *Foxe's Christian Martyrs of the World*, (Uhrichsville, OH: Barbour Publishing Inc., 2004), 181.

23. Roland H. Bainton, *Here I Stand: A Life of Martin Luther* (Nashville: Abingdon Press, 1978), 295. Though Luther distinguishes between punishment for heresy and sedition, it seems that there is an inescapable link, at least with the Anabaptists, between the two. If the Anabaptists were seditious it was because they were understood to be heretics. This says much about the connection between "right doctrine" and "good governance" during the sixteenth century.

24. Edmund Pries argues that just the refusal of oath-taking alone was enough to warrant suspicion that the articles were intended as a repudiation of civil society. See his "Oath Refusal in Zurich from 1525 to 1527: The Erratic Emergence of Anabaptist Practice," in Walter Klaassen, ed., *Anabaptists Revisited* (Scottdale: Herald Press, 1992), 65-84. In *The Legacy of Michael Sattler* (Scottdale: Herald Press, 1973), John Howard Yoder mentions the strong polemic against these articles by theologians of stature such as Huldreich Zwingli and John Calvin.

25. For a good introduction to the life and work known of Michael Sattler, see John Howard Yoder, *The Legacy of Michael Sattler* (Scottdale: Herald Press, 1973).

26. Cf. Phillip Melanchton's arguments against the "great lies" that Anabaptists and Catholic monks share in common in his *Loci Communes* in Oliver O'Donovan and Joan Lockwood O'Donovan's *From Irenaeus to Grotius: A Sourcebook in Christian Political Thought 100-1625* (Grand Rapids: Eerdmans, 1999), 652-61.

27. John Dillenberger, ed., *John Calvin: Selections from His Writings* (Atlanta: Scholars Press for the American Academy of Religion, 1975), 27.

28. Cf. Gregory, *Salvation at Stake*, 89, 319-20.

29. Such charges, while interesting (specifically because they pertain to charity), fail to take into account how seriously Anabaptists did exercise

punishment. To suffer the ban, I imagine, was no picnic. The critique against the Anabaptists also understands politics as behavior that owes its existence to temporal authorities rather than heavenly citizenship (because adherence to the latter implies an apolitical stance in the now). The charge of apoliticism is still rampant today. It is not that the Anabaptists of the sixteenth century wished to withdrawal from the world (where would they go?), but that their posture as a visibly separate people would reveal the genuine politics of the kingdom that would, hopefully, make possible the conversion of the parasitic forms of politics occupying the world. It is precisely in the "separatist" posture (in the sense of holiness as that which is "set apart") of the Anabaptist martyr that one finds not only the political representative of heaven but also the political outcasts of the temporal orders by which secular politics is founded.

30. George A. Lindbeck, *The Nature of Doctrine: Religion and Theology in a Postliberal Age* (Philadelphia: Westminster Press, 1984), 16.

31. Ibid.

32. In Lindbeck's view, a cognitive-propositionalist could have it both ways. That is, for the believer the host is the flesh of Christ, while for the unbeliever it is simply bread. Lindbeck's concern lies not so much with realism/antirealism as it does with the propositional form of the claim being made.

33. Given that a martyr is only a martyr because the church names her or him as such, is it not possible that, as with so many other things in history, the church has erred on this as well? For instance, if a Joan of Arc, in spite of previous hierarchical Catholic sentiments toward her, can be named a saint, can a saint, after further reflection, be relieved of her or his sainthood?

34. Lindbeck, *The Nature of* Doctrine, 17.

35. Ibid., 17.

36. Ibid., 18.

37. Ibid., 33.

38. Ibid.

39. Brag Gregory, though not specifically naming George Lindbeck, argues that such doctrinal contraries like transubstantiation, and infant baptism versus believer's baptism "were, are, and always will be irreconcilable, because their incompatibility turns strictly on logic." *Salvation at Stake*, 344.

40. Ibid., 64.

41. Ibid.

42. Ibid.

43. In the example above, many would instinctively argue for the former. However, we must follow Augustine and remember that it is "not the punishment, but the cause that makes the martyr." It is not enough to suffer punishment; rather, one must suffer punishment for the right reasons. All three traditions could point to their sufferings and find continuity with the bibli-

cal and early-church tradition, but as Augustine informed the Donatists, suffering is not a sufficient criterion for holiness. The flip side of Augustine's maxim is that it is employed to distinguish lawful prosecution from unjust persecution. If the punishment results from a just cause, then the one being punished is not being persecuted. Christian magistrates are merely fulfilling their duty to keep order. Therefore, in the scenario above, we cannot make a judgment in regards to an authentic martyrdom without knowing *why* this person was burned at the stake. However, Augustine's maxim is also limited in how much, precisely in the sixteenth century, work it can do. If it does turn out that the punished is really being persecuted, it still may not be enough to warrant a genuine martyrdom. If the persecutors' cry of "Jesus is Lord" is false, this does not necessarily make the victim's cry true. If the one at the stake is a participant in a tradition that does not rule out, *a priori*, capital punishment for heresy and/or sedition, that is, if a Protestant is burning a Catholic, yet the Catholic condones the killing of Protestants, then it is possible to claim, if one is an Anabaptist, that their cries of "Jesus is Lord" are false on both accounts.

44. Lindbeck, *The Nature of Doctrine*, 65.

45. Just because some refuse to persecute others does not mean that they embody Christian faithfulness. To be punished, even if the punished refuses to punish, is not sufficient in and of itself. What constitutes martyrdom is dying because of one's friendship with God, not just a commitment to nonviolence qua nonviolence (though much of the argument centers around whether or not one can call Jesus a friend and be anything other than nonviolent). Whether or not the practice of nonviolence is a necessary characteristic of the one to be named a martyr has been debatable since the advent of the rise of "military martyrs," beginning as early as the late fourth century. Traditionally, however, it has been understood that a martyr never commits any act of violence that would precipitate her own death. Karl Rahner, in his attempt to broaden the church's conception of martyrdom, begins by admitting that what has traditionally been understood as an act of martyrdom is the "free, tolerant acceptance of death for the sake of faith, except in the course of an active struggle as in the case of soldiers." "Dimensions of Martyrdom: A Plea for the Broadening of a Classical Concept," in *Concilium* 163, no. 3 (1983). For an interesting account of how some of the early church's nonviolent martyrs have turned into warrior martyrs to support later violent ideologies see chapter 3 of Joyce E. Salisbury's *The Blood of Martyrs: Unintended Consequences of Ancient Violence* (New York: Routledge, 2004).

46. Lindbeck, *The Nature of Doctrine*, 85.

47. Van Braght, *Martyrs Mirror*, 21.

48. Ibid., 27.

49. Ibid., 21. Van Braght also stated that there are two churches. Those

churches that are persecuting the Anabaptist churches are of Satan, while the Anabaptists and those who are likeminded in terms of baptism are of God. The Anabaptists, of course, were not alone in making this claim about the satanic nature of Catholics and Protestants, as they were often referred to as the "devil's martyrs."

50. Ibid.

51. Ibid., 22-27.

52. John Christian Wenger, ed., *The Complete Writings of Menno Simons* (Scottdale: Herald Press, 1956), 584-85. Simons qualified his harsh invective by stating that the "true and chosen children of God must not, no matter how heavily the cross may be laid over them by these people, be angry over them, but sincerely pity them . . . praying over their raging and cursed folly and blindness—for they know not what they do" (585).

53. Van Braght, *Martyrs Mirror*, 25. *Martyrs Mirror* continues by giving examples from the Old and New Testaments as well as moments within historical Christianity where at certain places and certain times, the church was hidden (24-26).

54. Ibid., 26.

55. Ibid.

56. The two forms of succession are predicated on each other because personal succession—the succession of one person by another—is only possible if doctrinal succession has occurred. A teacher of the gospel can be succeeded only by another whose teaching does not deviate from this gospel. For the Anabaptists, there had to be room for differences because the polygenetic nature of its origins did not make for the best circumstances to produce total unity of doctrine. What is crucial and shows itself in *Martyrs Mirror* is that differences can exist among the Anabaptists as long as what unites them is the understanding of a believer's baptism.

57. To make believer's baptism the key article and practice constitutive of Christianity narrows the possibility of not only authentic martyrdoms but authentic Christians. Despite my convictions regarding the "rightness" of believer's baptism, I believe that many people do live into their infant baptism and, for these Christians, another baptism *would* be a second and heretical baptism.

58. Wenger, *The Complete Writings of Menno Simons*, 44.

59. Ibid., 604. Emphasis added.

60. Ibid., 612.

61. Ibid.

62. Despite the jettisoning of the creeds indicative of much of contemporary Anabaptism, the sixteenth-century Anabaptists were not so quick to dismiss such a vital grammar of theological speech and affirmation. For further information, see Arnold Snyder's discussion of the creeds in first- and

second-generation Anabaptism in his *Anabaptist History and Theology: An Introduction* (Kitchener, Ont.: Pandora Press, 1995), 84-85, 365-66.

63. I believe this to be the very point the author of the *The Epistle of Mathetes to Diognetus* was making when he argued that Christians dwell in their own countries but only as sojourners. "Every foreign land is to them as their native country, and every land of their birth as a land of strangers." In *ANF* 1:26.

64. Cf. William T. Cavanaugh's "The City: Beyond Secular Parodies," in *Radical Orthodoxy: A New Theology*, eds. John Milbank, Catherine Pickstock, and Graham Ward (London and New York: Routledge, 1999), 182-200. The next chapter will delve further into his work.

65. *Martyrs Mirror* itself was written primarily for those Anabaptists who found themselves in situations of relative ease. Van Braght realized that toleration was far more dangerous than persecution. This was a tradition that viewed persecution as a necessary sign of the true church, and within only a century many Anabaptists found themselves in relative comfort. Gregory states it well: "Van Braght did not write for readers facing martyrdom. It was rather the rising tide of affluence and cultural assimilation that was killing Mennonites slowly, seductively, draining their spiritual identity." For any tradition that renders persecution as a visible sign of the authenticity of God's people, the lack of persecution clearly poses a problem. *Salvation at Stake*, 246-48.

66. Cited in C. Arnold Snyder's *Following in the Footsteps of Christ: The Anabaptist Tradition*, (Maryknoll, NY: Orbis Books, 2004), 166-67.

67. Ibid., 169.

68. According to W. H. C. Frend, Donatus never advocated retaliatory violence against the empire *Martrydom and Persecution in the Early Church*, 414. That some of his followers did need not necessarily reflect on his understanding of Christianity. *Martyrs Mirror* does claim Donatus as a kind of proto-Anabaptist, yet only to the extent that his teaching coincides with those things it deems good and true. Those things in which he erred, *Martyrs Mirror* does not defend. Van Braght, *Martyrs Mirror*, 155.

69. Chris K. Huebner argues against certain tendencies that attempt to fix and secure oneself against the risk of insecurity and claims that, following Gillian Rose, the "delicate task of discriminating between genuine and false martyrs" may be a task that necessarily remains "unfinished." See his *A Precarious Peace: Yoderian Explorations on Theology, Knowledge, and Identity* (Waterloo, Ontario & Scottdale, PA: Herald Press, 2006), 195.

70. Van Braght, *Martyrs Mirror*, 420-22. Also see John S. Oyer and Robert S. Kreider, eds., *Mirror of the Martyrs* (Intercourse, PA: Good Books, 1990), 72-73.

71. Cf. Stanley Hauerwas, *With the Grain of the Universe: The Church's Witness and Natural Theology* (Grand Rapids: Brazos Press, 2001), 205-44.

Chapter 4
City: Enduring Enoch

1. Cf. John Howard Yoder, *For the Nations: Essays Public and Evangelical* (Grand Rapids: Eerdmans, 1997). This will be a constant theme I will explore in this chapter.

2. For a thorough discussion of this ontology of peace as well as its embodiment in a space that rejects it, see John Milbank, *Theology and Social Theory: Beyond Secular Reason* (Oxford: Blackwell Publishers), 380-434, and *Being Reconciled: Ontology and Pardon* (London: Routledge, 2003) 26-43.

3. Cavanaugh, "The City: Beyond Secular Parodies," 182-200.

4. Augustine, *Concerning the City of God Against the Pagans*, trans. Henry Bettenson (London: Penguin Books, 1984), 15.1.

5. Ibid. Augustine also drew an analogy between the city of Enoch and Rome. He reminded his readers that Rome was also founded on the murder of a brother (15.5). Cyprian drew an even deeper connection, in terms of continuity with the martyrs, by arguing that Abel initiated martyrdom. Stephen may have been the first martyr, but his act is rooted historically to the offering of Abel to God (which resulted in the loss of Abel's life). Cyprian, *The Epistles of Cyprian*, in *ANF*, 5:348.

6. *City of God*, 15.1.

7. Ibid., 19.17.

8. Ibid. Emphasis added.

9. Ibid., 19.26. Despite its rebellion, Augustine did not demonize the earthly city. To demonize it would be wrong, given that God authorizes the powers of this world (Rom 13:1); yet not to recognize its fallen origins is to miss its significance. If we can trace our lineage back to Abel, we still have to reckon with the fact that Cain is our relative. Though the brothers belong to different cities, they are still brothers—that suggests an inescapable intermingling of the two cities. Just as Abel was not capable of escaping relations with his brother, so are Christians not capable of avoiding the earthly city.

10. Ibid., 13.16 Augustine actually equated the city of God with the church in this chapter; yet I think he made it abundantly clear throughout his work that the church is not the heavenly city. The church is a glimpse of the heavenly city as it makes its way to the eternal city.

11. Ibid., 14.28.

12. Ibid., 19.17.

13. In *Christian Doctrine*, 1.3-1.7 and 1.22.20-21, Augustine discusses the distinction between goods intended for use and goods to be enjoyed. His emphasis on the temporality of earthly goods should in no way tempt the Christian to approach creation (from trees, to nonhuman animals to human animals) as something to be merely exploited—as if these things had no relation to the trinitarian God. All of creation is good and should be

approached from the understanding that, precisely as pilgrims journeying through this world, we, of all people, should live with the utmost care in relation to what belongs completely to God. To disregard God's creation is to ignore that all creation groans for completion (Rom 8:22) and, in some mysterious way, only exists in relation to the triune God.

14. Graham Ward, *Cities of God* (London and New York: Routledge, 2000), 230.

15. Ibid.

16. Cavanaugh, "The City: Beyond Secular Parodies," 182-200.

17. Ibid., 182.

18. Ibid. Cavanaugh briefly defines the state as a "centralized and abstract power" that "holds a monopoly over physical coercion within a geographically defined territory" (183).

19. Ibid., 186.

20. Ibid.

21. Ibid., 187.

22. Ibid., 189.

23. Ibid.

24. Ibid.

25. This presumes that the soul is something that is internal, which may or may not be the case. I do think, however, that the common idiom of our culture makes this presumption and therefore I am, on this point, speaking in this vernacular.

26. Ibid., 190.

27. Graham Ward, "Why is the City so Important for Christian Theology?" *Cross Currents* 52, no. 4: 469.

28. In Torture and Eucharist Cavanaugh vividly reveals how the church loses any means of resisting tyrannical state practices when it complies with the myth that suggests the church is the keeper of the soul and the state, the body. He shows how the church in Chile successfully "disappeared" itself by buying into modernity's politics, therefore leaving itself without resources against the demonic principalities and powers as found under the Pinochet regime.

29. I imagine that most Christians would not claim that the state is their savior, though it is difficult to refute the reality that many pilgrims have made their home within the state. The large presence of Christians found in nation-state-operated militaries suggests that all we have in this world is this world. Abstract accounts of "freedom" and "justice" that underwrite much Christian involvement in the military assume that these conceptions are ends in themselves. No longer must Christians answer to the kind of freedom that comes with obedience to the One who demands that we sheathe our swords (John 18:10), deny ourselves, and pick up our

crosses (Luke 9:23); rather, freedom must be fought for in order to secure the continued existence of the state. Since the state ensures the survival of future generations, it must be protected as if our very lives depended on it. I am simply not convinced that such reasoning does not, ultimately, locate earthly existence as more than a temporal good.

30. Milbank, *Theology and Social Theory*, 391-92.

31. Cavanaugh, "The City: Beyond Secular Parodies," 193.

32. Augustine, *City of God*, 19.

33. Cavanaugh, "The City: Beyond Secular Parodies," 185.

34. I think it is clear that Augustine never celebrated the Constantinian synthesis as if it were some fruition of the promised kingdom. He continually argued that the earthly city of Rome remained in bondage to *amor sui*. Nevertheless, his use of imperial power against the Donatists represented a close merger between empire and church. It is possible to argue that such action was simply the practice of Jeremiah's command to seek the peace of the city, yet it could also be argued that such action was antithetical to Augustine's own thinking. Gerald Schlabach comments that Augustine forgot that God overcomes through a different kind of domination than humans. Just as Augustine was converted peaceably by God, so also must the church mirror God's patience through its efforts to maintain peace. For a critique of Augustine's way of correcting the Donatists, see Schlabach, "The Correction of the Augustinians: A Case Study in the Critical Appropriation of a Suspect Tradition," in *The Free Church and the Early Church*, ed. D. H. Williams (Grand Rapids: Eerdmans, 2002).

35. Cf. John Howard Yoder, *For the Nations: Essays Evangelical and Public* (Grand Rapids: Eerdmans, 1997), and Bruce W. Winter, *Seek the Welfare of the City: Christians as Benefactors and Citizens* (Grand Rapids: Eerdmans, 1994). Though Yoder and Winter both agree that the seeking of welfare of the city is necessary for Christians, they differ greatly in both the form and posture of how it is that Christians should seek the city's welfare.

36. Yoder, *For the Nations*, 51-78.

37. Gerald Schlabach, "The Christian Witness in the Earthly City: John H. Yoder as Augustinian Interlocutor." This comes from an unpublished paper delivered at the Believers Church Conference at the University of Notre Dame in March 2002.

38. John H. Yoder, "Exodus and Exile," *Cross Currents* 23, no. 3 (1974): 306 (emphasis his).

39. Yoder, *For the Nations*, 52. See also Yoder, *The Jewish-Christian Schism Revisted*, ed. Michael G. Cartwright and Peter Ochs (Grand Rapids: Eerdmans, 2003), 183-203. Ochs comments on Yoder's development of Diaspora as both a Jewish and a Christian calling by arguing that Yoder needed to be open to the possibility that, for the Jews, there are new and/or

different ways of being in the world than diasporic ones (204). Such a critique, it seems to me, risks forgetting the one thing that Jews and Christians share: the nomadic calling of Abraham.

40. Ibid., 53.

41. Yoder, "Exodus and Exile," 306, and *For the Nations*, 66-69.

42. Yoder, "Exodus and Exile," 307.

43. Ibid., 307.

44. That they were both saved is indeed a good thing though it is not the norm. Thousands of years of martyrs attest against making this a norm. This is, however, Yoder's point. In the cases of Joseph and Daniel (both saved) or in the cases of Polycarp and Dirk Willems (both martyred) the issue is faithfulness not effectiveness. Though, as apocalyptic people, Christians believe such witness to not be without effect, it nevertheless remains beyond our power to control how our witness will be received. All we can do is offer it.

45. Ibid., 307-8.

46. *The Epistle of Mathetes to Diognetus*, in *ANF*, 1:26.

47. John H. Yoder, "On Not Being in Charge," *The Jewish-Christian Schism Revisited: A Bundle of Old Essays* (Elkhart, IN: Shalom Desktop Publications, 1996), 138.

48. Augustine, *City of God*, 19.24.

49. In "What If There Had Been a Stronger Faith?" in *Christian Attitudes to War, Peace and Revolution: A Companion to Bainton* (distributed by Co-op Bookstore, Elkhart, IN, 1983), Yoder asked what it might have meant for Constantine to have undergone conversion and then have lived his life in radical obedience to Jesus. Yoder asked why God would not "be able to bless the believing obedience of a Caesar who, taking the risk of faith like any other believer, from his position of relative power, would love his enemies and do justice?" If the emperor's enemies triumphed over him, that usually happens anyway. The ruler might be elected out of office or assassinated, yet this too occurs. The converted ruler might ask that his people suffer for his convictions, but how does this differ from any non-Christian ruler? So Yoder did entertain God's ability to convert rulers, but he also wanted to know what it would look like if the ruler were to take *following* Jesus seriously (53-54).

50. Stanley Hauerwas, *The Peaceable Kingdom: A Primer in Christian Ethics* (Notre Dame: University of Notre Dame Press, 1983), 99-102.

51. Ibid.,100.

52. John Howard Yoder, *The Priestly Kingdom: Social Ethics as Gospel* (Notre Dame: University of Notre Dame Press, 1984), 11.

53. Ibid., 158-59.

54. Cavanaugh, "The City: Beyond Secular Parodies," 194-98. Anarchism does not mean either violence or chaos. When Joseph Proudhon coined the term *anarchist* he said, "By that I mean anything but disorder." Cf. Daniel

Guerin's short but concise introduction titled *Anarchism* (New York: Monthly Review Press, 1970) and his edited work *No Gods, No Masters*, vols. 1-2 (San Francisco: AK Press, 1998). It can be argued that since anarchism arises as a protest against the disorder of the nation-state, secular anarchists remain indebted to the state (inasmuch as their protest arises as a reaction to the state). The church, it seems, may be anarchical because it does not need to react against either the order or disorder of the state to know who she is. The church has stronger possibilities for practicing anarchy than those whose position colludes with the very object of their protest.

55. Yoder, *For the Nations*, 33-34.

56. Ibid., 69.

57. This is not an uncontested claim. Jewish scholar Peter Ochs takes Yoder to task in *The Jewish-Christian Schism Revisited* for suggesting that this must be the normative way of being for God's people in the world. Ochs claims that just as "Yoder has encouraged us to imagine the past in new ways, so must we post-liberal Jews ask our newfound Anabaptist friends to imagine with us new ways for Israel's future in a post-modern world. This means, as well, new ways for western economics and politics, rather than just new forms of the old western dichotomy between the ways of power and the ways of powerlessness" (204).

58. Graham Ward, "Why is the City so Important for Christian Theology?" *Cross Currents*, 52, no. 4: 464.

59. John Milbank, *Theology and Social Theory: Beyond Secular Reason* (Oxford: Basil Blackwell, 1991), 392. Emphasis added.

60. Paul S. Fiddes, *The Promised End: Eschatology in Theology and Literature* (Oxford: Blackwell Publishers, 2000), 283.

61. Ibid.

62. Ibid., 284.

63. Ibid., 287.

Chapter 5
Biography: Oscar Romero

1. My most significant point of conflict with those who influenced and are influenced by Romero (liberation theologians in general) is the manner in which we narrate the so-called secular and how this shapes how we think about faith/politics. Their work represents what has been generally called "politicized theology," while I am working under the notion of a "theological politic." The major difference between the two is that the former, despite its intention to challenge the structures of the status quo, assumes the legitimacy of the autonomy of the temporal and is led to presume the very accounts of society that have legitimated it—making a theological critique dubious. A theological politic, on the other hand, does not assume any space

free of God (that would be nihilism—or nothingness) and narrates these "invented spaces" (the secular) as what they are—just other mythoi. For more on this see John Milbank's critique of political theology in *Theology and Social Theory*, 9-26, 206-55. Romero is interesting in this regard because, even though he did not have the resources to speak in terms of theological politics per se, his obedience to Jesus, coupled with his disinterest in what one calls such a politic, embodied a politic that actually renders the political theology model of liberation theology problematic.

2. For an account of, and against, the "manipulation theory'"(that is, Romero was manipulated by sources outside of genuine ecclesial boundaries), see Jon Sobrino, *Witnesses to the Kingdom: The Martyrs of El Salvador and the Crucified Peoples* (Maryknoll, NY: Orbis Books, 2003), 46-53.

3. I am convinced that Romero's status as an official martyr will be recognized in the near future. When it is, this will neither negate my attraction toward his life nor my argument against the church's tendency to adopt alien politics. It will simply confirm that, on occasion, we do get things right—and that is a good thing.

4. See Marie Dennis, Renny Golden, and Scott Wright's introduction to *Oscar Romero: Reflections on His Life and Writings* (Maryknoll, NY: Orbis Books, 2000), 7-17.

5. For more on the adverse reaction to Romero's ordination, see chapter 2 of James R. Brockman, *Romero: A Life* (Maryknoll, NY: Orbis Books, 2002), 33-61.

6. For an in-depth treatment of the consequences of the conference in Medellin as well as, quite possibly, the most thorough-going theology that came out of it, see Gustavo Gutierrez, *A Theology of Liberation: History, Politics, and Salvation* (Maryknoll, NY: Orbis Books, 1988).

7. Though Romero, like any faithful Christian, favored the way of peace, he was not a committed pacifist. He never declared that Catholic soldiers in El Salvador should throw down their weapons. He did claim that soldiers should never obey an order that is contrary to the will of God, yet he was never entirely clear if an order to kill must only be disobeyed when it comes to killing a member of the church, not necessarily one's enemy. For more on Romero's understanding of justifiable violence see Jon Sobrino, *Jesus the Liberator: A Historical-Theological View* (Maryknoll, NY: Orbis Books, 2001), 212-14. Romero distinguished the differences between certain kinds of violence and, despite granting an adamant preference for nonviolence, argued that violence as a form of self-defense might be employed, but only as a last resort. Cf. Archbishop Oscar Romero, *The Voice of the Voiceless: Four Pastoral Letters and Other Statements*, trans. Michael J. Walsh (Maryknoll, NY: Orbis Books, 2002), 109-10.

8. Dennis, Golden, and Wright, *Oscar Romero*, 26.

9. Susan Bergman, ed., *Martyrs: Contemporary Writers on Modern Lives of Faith* (New York: HarperCollins, 1996), 59.

10. Robert Ellsberg, *All Saints: Daily Reflections on Saints, Prophets, and Witnesses for our Time* (New York: Crossroad Publishing Company, 2000), 114.

11. Brockman, *Romero*, 10.

12. Sobrino, *Witness to the Kingdom*, 17.

13. For an account of Paul that interprets this experience as calling from within Judaism rather than a conversion from without see Krister Stendahl, *Paul Among the Jews and Gentiles and Other Essays* (Minneapolis: Augsburg Fortress Press, 1997).

14. I am following the work of William James McClendon whose understanding of Wittgenstein suggests that our actions are only intelligible in light of, not different chains of reasoning, but the picture we have of the world. See his *Systematic Theology*, vol. 2, *Doctrine* (Nashville: Abingdon Press, 1994), 75-77.

15. Brockman, *Romero*, 10.

16. Dennis, Golden, and Wright, *Oscar Romero*, 41.

17. Brockman, *Romero*, 17.

18. Ibid., 20.

19. Dennis, Golden, and Wright, *Oscar Romero*, 19.

20. Ibid., 35.

21. Ibid., 32.

22. Oscar Romero, *The Violence of Love*, 12.

23. Even after his murder, Romero's request went ignored. One week after his death, the United States appropriated almost six million dollars in military aid to the Salvadoran government. Within a twelve-year period, the United States averaged one million dollars a day in aid—the most to any region save the Middle East. Cf. Dennis, Golden, and Wright, *Oscar Romero*, 94.

24. Ibid., 65.

25. Brockman, Romero, 241-42. Emphasis added.

26. Ibid., 244-45.

27. Sobrino, *Witnesses to the Kingdom*, 42. Sobrino implies that it is not enough to merely give cognitive assent to the notion of "God"; rather, belief implicitly entails a life of obedience that renders such belief believable.

28. Peter also claimed that we are to "accept the authority of every human institution, whether of the emperor as supreme, or of governors" (1 Pet 2:13). The issue for Christians is not whether we submit to their authority, as Jesus freely submitted to the Roman Empire, but how our submission, while remaining obedient to Christ, takes on a revolutionary character. Also, if Paul's words are the final say on how we are to behave in light of government authority then his behavior is a wonderful exegetical resource for interpretation. He was con-

stantly on the run, arrested several times and executed by the empire. For a more thorough account of these passages see John Howard Yoder's chapters "Revolutionary Subordination" and "Let Every Soul Be Subject: Romans 13 and the Authority of the State," in *The Politics of Jesus* (Grand Rapids: William B. Eerdmanns Publishing Co., 1998).

29. Dennis, Golden, and Wright, *Oscar Romero*, 21.

30. Romero, *The Violence of Love*, 140.

31. Ibid., 88.

32. William T. Cavanaugh, *Theopolitical Imagination: Discovering the Liturgy as a Political Act in an Age of Global Consumerism* (London: T & T Clark, 2002), 122.

33. It was public knowledge that Romero would be where he was when he was murdered. His serving of the mass at the chapel of the Divina Providencia hospital, where only a few people surrounded him, made him easy pickings for an assassination.

34. Dennis, Golden, and Wright, *Oscar Romero*, 86.

35. Ibid., 98.

36. Ibid., 90.

37. Chenu, *Book of Christian Martyrs*, 64.

38. Lawrence S. Cunningham, *The Meaning of the Saints* (San Francisco: Harper & Row Publishers, 1980), 65.

39. Ibid., 140. Cunningham notes that many of these Jesuits are now canonized.

40. Romero, *Voice of the Voiceless*, 67. He also argues that the rift between the temporal and the eternal, the religious and the secular, and the world and God displays a corruption of the unity that God has ordained.

41. Chenu, *Book of Christian Martyrs*, 87-88.

42. Dennis, Golden, & Wright, *Oscar Romero*, 98-99. Emphasis added.

43. Romero, *The Violence of Love*, 135.

44. Romero, perhaps in an attempt to counter the claims against him about being politically subversive, often claimed that he was not delving into the arena of politics but was simply attempting to respond to the neediness of his people in a way congruent with the gospel. I too do not think of Christianity as a mere supplement to a life of politics; rather, Christianity is a politic that offers an alternative to every form of politics at work within the world. This is what I mean by the phrase "inherent politics of the church." Christians are not to go into the world with their Christianity and attempt to mingle with the politics of the world as if this is what it means to be political, but by simply being Christians they are already embodying the kind of life that is inescapably political.

45. Oscar Romero, *The Violence of Love*, comp. and trans. James R. Brockman, SJ (Farmington: Plough Publishing House, 1998), 205.

46. That this is so provides one more instance that displays the parasitical nature of earthly accounts of citizenship. Citizenship in heaven is neither premised upon nor made possible by those who would reject such citizenship; rather, this citizenship is contingent upon participation in the triune God. That the earthly city requires an account of those excluded from it to gain its own intelligibility simply reinforces how the temporal city assumes an ontology of violence that imagines an antagonism at work within creation.

47. Tertullian, *The Chaplet, or De Corona*, in *ANF*, 3:93.

48. Ibid.

Epilogue
Gift—A Non-sacrificial Economy

1. David Bentley Hart, *The Beauty of the Infinite: The Aesthetics of Christian Truth* (Grand Rapids: Eerdmans, 2003), 440.

2. Ibid., 441.

3. The specific definition of *tragedy* is far more complex than stated here, though this does give a rendering of what is often meant when the word is employed. For a comprehensive study of the various meanings of *tragedy*, see Terry Eagleton, *Sweet Violence: The Idea of the Tragic* (Oxford: Blackwell Publishing, 2003). I am not attempting to rob people who have suffered horrible crimes or accidents from any meaning they may or may not have attached to the act (as a means of coping with the ongoing depravity of our fallen natures and pre-restored creation); I am simply noting that the language used for a random act of killing or, for example, one who suffers at the hands of a drunk driver, is not the same language used for one who directly suffers death due to his or her confession of Christ and another's hatred of this confession (and the simultaneous implications of such a confession).

4. See David Toole, *Waiting for Godot in Sarajevo: Theological Reflections on Nihilism, Tragedy and Apocalypticism* (Boulder: Westview Press, 1998) for an account of how the language of tragedy is at odds with the apocalyptic world of Christianity.

5. For an in-depth study of the ontology of violence underwriting secularism, see John Milbank, *Theology and Social Theory*, 278-321.

6. Hart, *The Beauty of the Infinite*, 346.

7. See my essay "Re-thinking Jon Sobino's Thinking Through Martyrdom," in *Mennonite Quarterly Review* 78, no. 2 (April 2004), for an extended argument against the idea of Jesus as a martyr.

8. Hart, *The Beauty of the Infinite*, 344. Catherine Pickstock reminds us that one of the many different words used for gift in the liturgy is not just *donum* but is *sacrificium*, which she claims grants a dual nature to the notion of gift, one as being gratuitous and the other sacrificial. Pickstock ties all gifts, that of creation, resurrection, martyrdom, the Eucharist, etc.,

to the first gift: the incarnation. Catherine Picskstock, *After Writing: On the Liturgical Consummation of Philosophy* (Malden: Blackwell Publishers, 2000), 240.

9. Ibid., 441-42.

10. Balthasar Hubmaier, an advocate of the view that the Eucharist is symbolic, claims that even though the elements are "outward symbols of an inward Christian nature" this does not lessen the material implications of this meal. He states, "Thus as the body and blood of Christ became my body and blood on the cross, so likewise shall my body and blood become the body and blood of my neighbor, and in time of need, theirs become my body and blood, or we cannot boast at all to be Christians. This is the will of Christ in the Supper." H. Wayne Pipkin and John Howard Yoder, eds., *Balthasar Hubmaier: Theologian of Anabaptism* (Scottdale: Herald Press, 1989), 75-76.

11. For a more detailed account of how the Eucharist makes martyrdom possible as well how the ability to produce martyrs is what makes participation in the Eucharist an intelligible act, see my essay "Martyrdom and Eating Jesus: Two Neglected Practices?" in *The Conrad Grebel Review* 22:1 (Winter 2004): 71-86.

12. Cited in Cavanaugh, "The City: Beyond Secular Parodies," 195.

13. Cavanaugh, "The City: Beyond Secular Parodies," 196.

14. Catherine Pickstock, *After Writing: On the Litrugical Consummation of Philosophy* (Oxford: Blackwell Publishers, 2000), 244.

15. Hart, *The Beauty of the Infinite*, 351.

16. Pipkin and Yoder, *Balthasar Hubmaier*, 407.

17. This is why the martyrdom of Dietrich Bonhoeffer is so difficult to speak well about. Bonhoeffer was not killed because he was "being" Jesus as a response to Hitler, but precisely in abandoning Jesus, by trying to assassinate another human being, Bonhoeffer proved Jesus' maxim: "Those who live by the sword die by the sword." What makes this case so complex is the life and writings of Bonhoeffer prior to his involvement in an assassination plot as well as his reflections during his time awaiting his punishment. For a detailed defense of the martyrdom of Bonhoeffer, see Craig Slane, *Bonhoeffer as Martyr: Social Responsibility and Modern Christian Commitment* (Grand Rapids: Brazos Press, 2004). Slane is onto something when he argues against the modern bifurcation between politics and religion, yet in arguing against this dualism he adopts the politics of modernity, or politicized theology (as opposed to theo-politics). He is right to argue for the political implications of the gospel (if one can even separate the gospel from its implications), but is wrong to think that any political involvement that seems right and noble is necessarily the politics of Jesus.

18. Irenaeus, *Against Heresies*, 1:490.

Bibliography

Augustine, *Concerning the City of God Against the Pagans*, trans. Henry Bettenson. London: Penguin Books, 1984.

Bainton, Roland H. *Here I Stand: A Life of Martin Luther*. Nashville: Abingdon Press, 1978.

Bergman, Susan, ed., *Martyrs: Contemporary Writers on Modern Lives of Faith*. New York: HarperCollins, 1996.

Berry, Wendell. "The Mad Farmer Liberation Front," in *Context: A Quarterly of Humane Sustainable Culture*, Fall/Winter 1991.

Bloom, Harold. *The American Religion: The Emergence of a Post-Christian Nation*. New York: Simon & Schuster, 1992.

Bowersock, Gary. *Martyrdom and Rome*. Cambridge: Cambridge University Press, 2002.

Braght, Thieleman J. van. *The Martyrs Mirror or The Bloody Theater of the Defenseless Christians*. Second ed., 23rd printing. Scottdale: Herald Press, 2001.

Brockman, James R. *Romero: A Life*. Maryknoll, N.Y.: Orbis Books, 2002.

Brown, Peter. *The Body and Society: Men, Women, and Sexual Renunciation in Early Christianity*. New York: Columbia University Press, 1988.

———. *Augustine of Hippo*. Berkeley: University of California Press, 1969.

Carette, Jeremy, and Richard King. *Selling Spirituality: The Silent Takeover of Religion*. New York: Routledge, 2005.

Cavanaugh, William T. *Torture and Eucharist: Theology, Politics and the Body of Christ*. Oxford: Blackwell Publishers, 1998.

———. *Theopolitical Imagination: Discovering the Liturgy as a Political Act in an Age of Global Consumerism*. London: T & T Clark, 2002.

Chenu, Bruno, et al. *The Book of Christian Martyrs*. Trans. John Bowden. London: SCM Press, 1990.

Christo, Gus George. *Martyrdom According to John Chrysostom: To*

Live is Christ, To Die is Gain. Lewiston, NY: Mellen University Press, 1997.

Clapp, Rodney. *A Peculiar People: The Church as Culture in a Post-Christian Society*. Downers Grove, Ill.: InterVarsity Press, 1996.

Cunningham, Lawrence S. *The Meaning of the Saints*. San Franciso: Harper & Row, 1980.

Dennis, Marie, Renny Golden, and Scott Wright. *Oscar Romero: Reflections on His Life and Writings*. Maryknoll, N.Y.: Orbis Books, 2000.

Dillenberger, John. *John Calvin: Selections from His Writings*. Atlanta: Scholar Press for the American Academy of Religion, 1975.

Driver, John. *How Christians Made Peace with War: Early Christian Understandings of War*. Scottdale: Herald Press, 1988.

Dyck, Cornelius J. "The Suffering Church in Anabaptism." *Mennonite Quarterly Review* 59, no. 1 (1985).

Eagleton, Terry. *Sweet Violence: The Idea of the Tragic*. Oxford: Blackwell Publishing, 2003.

Ellsberg, Robert. *All Saints: Daily Reflections on Saints, Prophets, and Witnesses for Our Time*. New York: Crossroad Publishing, 2000.

Eusebius, *The History of the Church from Christ to Constantine*. Trans. G. A. Williamson. Ed. Andrew Louth. London: Penguin Books, 1985.

Fiddes, Paul S. *The Promised End: Eschatology in Theology and Literature*. Oxford: Blackwell Publishers, 2000.

Foucault, Michel. *Discipline and Punish: The Birth of the Prison*. Trans. Alan Sheridan. New York: Vintage, 1994.

Fox, Robin Lane. *Pagans and Christians*. New York: Alfred A. Knopf, 1989.

Foxe, John. *Foxe's Christian Martyrs of the World*. Uhrichsville, Ohio: Barbour Publishing Inc., 2004.

Frend, W. H. C. *Martyrdom and Persecution in the Early Church: A Study of Conflict from the Maccabees to Donatus*. Garden City, N.Y.: Anchor Books, 1967.

Gonzalez, Justo L. *The Story of Christianity*. Vol. 1, *The Early Church to the Dawn of The Reformation*. San Francisco: HarperCollins, 1984.

Gregory, Brad. *Salvation at Stake: Christian Martyrdom in Early Modern Europe*. Cambridge: Harvard University Press, 1999.

Guerin, Daniel. *Anarchism*. New York: Monthly Review Press, 1970.

————. *No Gods, No Masters: An Anthology of Anarchism.* Vol. 1. Trans. Paul Sharkey. San Francisco: AK Press, 1998.

Gutierrez, Gustavo. *A Theology of Liberation: History, Politics, and Salvation.* Maryknoll, N.Y.: Orbis Books, 1998.

Hammond, David M., ed. *Theology and Lived Christianity.* Mystic, CT: Twenty-Third Publications, 2000.

Hart, David Bentley. *The Beauty of the Infinite: The Aesthetics of Christian Truth.* Grand Rapids: Eerdmans, 2003.

Hauerwas, Stanley. *With the Grain of the Universe: The Church's Witness and Natural Theology.* Grand Rapids: Brazos Press, 2001.

————. *Sanctify Them in the Truth: Holiness Exemplified.* Nashville: Abingdon, 1998.

————. *The Peaceable Kingdom: A Primer in Christian Ethics.* Notre Dame, Ind.: University of Notre Dame Press, 1983.

Huebner, Chris K. "Between Victory and Victimhood: Reflections on Martyrdom and Culture" *Direction: A Mennonite Brethren Forum* 34, no. 2 (2005).

————. *A Precarious Peace: Yoderian Explorations on Theology, Knowledge, and Identity.* Scottdale: Herald Press, 2006.

Hummell, Edelhard L. *The Concept of Martyrdom According to St. Cyprian of Carthage.* Washington, D.C.: The Catholic University of America Press, 1946.

Isin, Engin F. *Being Political: Geneaologies of Citizenship.* Minneapolis: University of Minnesota Press, 2002.

Kierkegaard, Søren. *The Journals of Kierkegaard.* Trans. Alexander Dru. New York: Harper Torch Books, 1959.

Lactantius. *De Mortibus Persecutorum.* Ed. and trans. J. L. Creed. Oxford: Clarendon Press, 1984.

Laytham, D. Brent, ed. *God is Not . . . Religious, Nice, One of Us, An American, A Capitalist.* Grand Rapids: Brazos Press, 2004.

Lindbeck, George A. *The Nature of Doctrine: Religion and Theology in a Postliberal Age.* Philadelphia: Westminster Press, 1984.

Lysaught, M. Therese. "Witnessing Christ in Their Bodies: Martyrs and Ascetics as Doxological Disciples." *The Annual of the Society of Christian Ethics* 20 (2000).

Mayer, Wendy, and Pauline Allen. *John Chyrsostom.* London: Routledge, 2000.

McClendon, William J. *Systematic Theology.* Vol. 2, *Doctrine.* Nashville: Abingdon, 1994.

McParlan, Paul. *The Eucharist Makes the Church.* Edinburgh: T&T Clark, 1993.

Meecham, Henry G., trans. *The Epistle to Diognetus.* Manchester: Manchester University Press, 1949.

Melino, Livio. *Sharing in Christ's Virtues: For a Renewal of Moral Theology in Light of Veritatis Splendor.* Trans. William E. May. Washington, D.C.: The Catholic University of America Press, 2001.

Milbank, John. *Being Reconciled: Ontology and Pardon.* London: Routledge, 2003.

———. *Theology and Social Theory: Beyond Secular Reason.* Oxford: Blackwell Publishers, 1999.

Milbank, John, Catherine Pickstock, and Graham Ward. *Radical Orthodoxy: A New Theology.* London: Routledge, 2000.

Miller, Patricia Cox. "Desert Asceticism and 'The Body from Nowhere,'" *Journal of Early Christian Studies* 2 (1994).

Musurillo, Herbert, ed. *The Acts of the Martyrs.* Oxford: Clarendon Press, 1972.

Nicholson, O. P. "Flight from Persecution as Imitation of Christ." *Journal of Theological Studies* 40 (1989): 48-65.

Nietzsche, Friedrich. *Beyond Good and Evil: Prelude to a Philosophy of the Future.* New York: Vintage, 1989.

O'Donovan, Oliver. *The Desire of the Nations: Rediscovering the Roots of Political Theology.* Cambridge: Cambridge University Press, 1999.

O'Donovan, Oliver, and Joan Lockwood O'Donovan, eds. *From Irenaeus to Grotius: A Sourcebook in Christian Political Thought 100-1625.* Grand Rapids: Eerdmans, 1999.

Origen. *An Exhortation to Martyrdom, Prayer, and Selected Works.* Trans. Rowan Greer. New York: Paulist Press, 1979.

Oyer, John S, and Robert S. Kreider, eds. *Mirror of the Martyrs.* Intercourse, Pa.: Good Books, 1990.

Paolucci, Henry. *The Political Writings of St. Augustine.* Washington, D.C.: Gateway Editions, 1962.

Perkins, Judith. *The Suffering Self: Pain and Narrative Representation in the Early Christian Era.* London: Routledge, 1995.

Pickstock, Catherine. *After Writing: On the Liturgical Consummation of Philosophy.* Oxford: Blackwell Publishers, 2000.

Pipkin, H. Wayne, and John Howard Yoder, eds. *Balthasar Hubmaier: Theologian of Anabaptism.* Scottdale: Herald Press, 1989.

Prokes, Mary Timothy, FSE. *Toward a Theology of the Body*. Grand Rapids: Eerdmans, 1996.

Quaster, Johannes, and Joseph C. Plumpe, eds. *Ancient Christian Writers*. No. 19, *Prayer and Exhortation to Martyrdom*. Trans. John J. O'Meara. Westminster: The Newman Press, 1954.

Roberts, Alexander, and James Donaldson, eds. *Ante-Nicene Fathers*. Vol. 1, *The Apostolic Fathers, Justin Martyr, Irenaeus*. Peabody, Mass.: Hendrickson Publishers, 1999.

———. *The Ante-Nicene Fathers*. Vol. 2, *Fathers of the Second Century*. Grand Rapids: Eerdmans, 1967.

———. *The Ante-Nicene Fathers*. Vol. 3. Buffalo: The Christian Literature Publishing Company, 1885.

———. *The Ante-Nicene Fathers*. Vol. 4. Buffalo: Christian Literature Publishing Company, 1885.

———. *The Ante-Nicene Christian Library*. Vol. 8. Edinburgh: T&T Clark, 1868.

Romero, Oscar. *The Violence of Love*. Comp. and trans. James R. Brockman, S. J. Farmington, Penn: Plough Publishing House, 1998.

———. *The Voice of the Voiceless: Four Pastoral Letters and Other Statements*. Trans. Michael J. Walsh. Maryknoll, N.Y.: Orbis Books, 2002.

Salisbury, Joyce E. *The Blood of the Martyrs: Unintended Consequences of Ancient Violence*. New York: Routledge, 2004.

———. *Perpetua's Passion: The Death and Memory of a Young Roman Woman*. New York: Routledge, 1997.

Scarry, Elaine. *The Body in Pain: The Making and Unmaking of the World*. Oxford: Oxford University Press, 1985.

Schlabach, Gerald. "The Christian Witness in the Earthly City: John H. Yoder as Augustinian Interlocutor." From an unpublished paper delivered at the Believers Church Conference at the University of Notre Dame, March 2002.

Schopp, Ludwig, ed. *The Fathers of the Church*. Trans. Gerald Walsh. New York: Christian Heritage, 1948.

Shakespeare, William. *The Complete Works of Shakespeare*. Ed. W. J. Craig. New York: Oxford University Press.

Shaw, Brent D. "Body/Power/Identity: Passions of the Martyrs." *Journal of Early Christian Studies* 4, no. 3 (Fall 1996).

Shaw, Teresa M. *The Burden of the Flesh: Fasting and Sexuality in Early Christianity*. Minneapolis: Fortress Press, 1998.

Simons, Menno. *The Complete Writings of Menno Simons.* Scottdale: Herald Press, 1956.

Slane, Craig. *Bonhoeffer as Martyr: Social Responsibility and Modern Christian Commitment.* Grand Rapids: Brazos Press, 2004.

Snyder, C. Arnold. *Anabaptist History and Theology: An Introduction.* Kitchener, Ont.: Pandora Press, 1995.

———. *Following in the Footsteps of Christ: The Anabaptist Tradition.* Maryknoll, N.Y: Orbis Books, 1998.

Sobrino, Jon. *Spirituality of Liberation: Toward Political Holiness.* Trans. Robert R. Barr. Maryknoll, N.Y.: Orbis Books, 1998.

———. *Jesus the Liberator: A Historical Theological View.* Trans. Paul Burns and Francis McDonagh. Maryknoll, N.Y.: Orbis Books, 2001.

———. *Witnesses to the Kingdom: The Martyrs of El Salvador and the Crucified Peoples.* Maryknoll, N.Y.: Orbis Books, 2003.

Stauffer, Ethelbert. "The Anabaptist Theology of Martyrdom." *Mennonite Quarterly Review* 19, no. 3 (1945).

Stendahl, Krister. *Paul Among the Jews and Gentiles and Other Essays.* Minneapolis: Augsburg Fortress Press, 1997.

Thompson, Leonard L. "The Martyrdom of Polycarp: Death in the Roman Games." *The Journal of Religion* 82 (2002).

Tilley, Maureen A. *Donatist Martyr Stories: The Church in Conflict in Roman North Africa.* Liverpool: Liverpool University Press, 1996.

———. "The Ascetic Body and the (Un)Making of the World of the Martyr." *Journal of The American Academy of Religion* 59, no. 3: 471.

Toole, David. *Waiting for Godot in Sarajevo: Theological Reflections on Nihilism, Tragedy, and Apocalypticism.* Boulder, Colo.: Westview Press, 1998.

Walker, Caroline Bynum. *The Resurrection of the Body in Western Christianity, 200-1336.* New York: Columbia University Press, 1995.

Ward, Benedicta. *The Sayings of the Desert Fathers.* Kalamazoo, Mich.: Cistercian Publications, 1975.

Ward, Graham. *Cities of God.* London: Routledge, 2000.

———. "Why is the City so Important for Christian Theology?" *Cross Currents,* 52, no. 4 (Winter 2003).

Water, Mark, ed. *The New Encyclopedia of Christian Martyrs.* Grand Rapids: Baker, 2001.

Wenger, John Christian, ed., *The Complete Writings of Menno Simons*. Scottdale: Herald Press, 1956.

Wiedemann, Thomas. *Emperors and Gladiators*. New York: Routledge, 1992.

Williams, D. H., ed. *The Free Church and the Early Church*. Grand Rapids: Eerdmans, 2002.

Winter, Bruce W. *Seek the Welfare of the City: Christians as Benefactors and Citizens*. Grand Rapids: Eerdmans, 1994.

Yoder, John Howard. *The Politics of Jesus: Vicit Agnus Noster*. Grand Rapids: Eerdmans, 1994.

———. *The Royal Priesthood*. Ed. Michael G. Cartwright. Scottdale: Herald Press, 1998.

———. *The Priestly Kingdom: Social Ethics as Gospel*. Notre Dame: University of Notre Dame Press, 1984.

———. *For the Nations: Essays Evangelical and Public*. Grand Rapids: Eerdmans, 1997.

———. *The Jewish Christian Schism Revisited*. Ed. Michael G. Cartwright and Peter Ochs. Grand Rapids: Eerdmans, 2003.

———. *The Legacy of Michael Sattler*. Scottdale: Herald Press, 1973.

———. "What if There Had Been a Stronger Faith?" in *Christian Attitudes to War, Peace and Revolution: A Companion to Bainton*. Distrib. by Mennonite Co-op Bookstore, Elkhart, Ind., 1983.

———. "On Not Being in Charge." *The Jewish-Christian Schism Revisited: A Bundle of Old Essays*. Elkhart, Ind.: Shalom Desktop Publications, 1996.

———. "Exodus and Exile." *Cross Currents* 23, no. 3 (1974).

York, Tripp. "Rethinking Jon Sobrino's 'Thinking Through Martyrdom.'" *Mennonite Quarterly Review* 78, no. 2 (April 2004).

———. "Martyrdom and Eating Jesus: Two Neglected Practices?" *The Conrad Grebel Review*, 22, no. 1 (Winter 2004).

Young, Robin. *In Procession Before the Word: Martyrdom as Public Liturgy in Early Christianity*. Milwaukee: Marquette University Press, 2001.

Zweig, Stephan. *Jeremiah: A Drama in Nine Scenes*. Trans. Eden and Cedar Paul. New York: Thomas Seltzer, 1922.

Index

aceticism, 57-58, 70
agon, 51
Ambrose, 35
amor; sui, 104-5, 178n; *dei*, 104-5
amphitheatre, 28, 33, 50; *see also* arena
Anabaptist, 24, 71, 75, 77-83, 88-95, 98, 100, 115, 169n, 171-75n, 180n
anarchism, 116, 143, 179-80n
Apprice, John, 80
arena, 28, 30, 32-35, 39, 40, 45, 49, 53, 56, 59, 62, 160n; *see also* amphitheatre
askesis, 58
Athanasius, 150
Attalus, 38
Augustine, 19-20, 24, 49, 73-74, 76, 100, 102-5, 107, 110-12, 169-70n, 172-73n
Augustine of Hippo, 18
Babylon, 103, 112-13, 115-16
Bainton, Roland H., 171n
baptism, 18-19, 21-23, 30, 40-44, 56-57, 62, 66, 77, 81, 92-93, 95, 125, 162-63n, 174n; of blood, 30, 43-44, 92-93; *see also* martyrdom; infant, 79; second baptism, 23, 30, 43-45, 50, 80
Becket, Thomas, 135, 151
Bergman, Susan, 182n
Berrigan, Daniel and Phillip, 139
Berry, Wendell, 145

blood-witness, 21-22, 45, 158-59n; *see also* martyrdom
Bloom, Harold, 164n
body politic, 23, 37, 58
Bonhoeffer, Dietrich, 20, 185n
Borgonovo, Mauricio, 131
Bowersock, Gary, 158n
Bramley-Moore, William, 21, 158n
Brockman, James R., 181-83n
Brown, Peter, 74, 165n, 169n
Bynum, Caroline Walker, 65-66, 70
Caecilian, 72, 76
Caecilius, 67-69
Caesar, 31, 40, 179n
Calvin, John, 82, 171n
Campion, Edmund, 80
Carette, Jeremy, 159n
Carter, Jimmy, 132
castra caelestia, 40
catechumens, 39, 41, 43, 162n
Catherine of Siena, 139
Catholic, 24, 39, 73-75, 78-82, 85, 88, 90, 95-96, 115, 129, 169-70n, 172-74n, 181n
Cavanaugh, William T., 57, 100, 107-10, 116, 136, 151-52, 158-59n, 166n, 170n, 175n, 183n
charity, 20, 40, 82, 88, 110, 171n
Charles V, 71
Chavez, Archbishop Luis, 124-25
Chenu, Bruno, 164n, 166n, 183n
Christ, 35-36, 38, 47, 77-78, 125, 129, 133-40, 148, 152, 154; body of 22, 39, 41, 57, 91,

The Author

Tripp York is a Visiting Assistant Professor of Religious Studies and serves on the committee for Non-Violence Studies at Elon University in North Carolina. His writings on Christian martyrdom have been published in multiple journals and magazines. He has a chapter in *Witness of the Body: The Past, Present and Future of Christian Martyrdom*, edited by Michael L. Budde and Karen Scott (Eerdmans, forthcoming, 2008).

York earned a PhD in Historical Theology and Ethics at Garrett-Evangelical Theological Seminary in 2006 and earlier had studied at Duke University and Trevecca Nazarene University. An actor and a lighting designer in a local theater where he lives in Burlington, North Carolina, York attends a Mennonite church in Graham, North Carolina.